EFFECTIVENESS OF REHABILITATION IN PATIENTS WHO HAVE HAD A RE-STROKE

(monograph)

SALOMOVA NILUFAR KAHHOROVNA

© Taemeer Publications LLC
Effectiveness of rehabilitation in patients who have had a re-stroke
by: Salomova Nilufar Kahhorovna
Edition: August '2023
Publisher:
Taemeer Publications LLC (Michigan, USA / Hyderabad, India)

ISBN 978-93-5872-128-7

© Taemeer Publications

Book	:	Effectiveness of rehabilitation in patients who have had a re-stroke
Author	:	Salomova Nilufar Kahhorovna
Publisher	:	Taemeer Publications
Year	:	'2023
Pages	:	218
Title Design	:	*Taemeer Web Design*

Bukhara – 2023.

Author: Salomova N.Q -PhD, Assistant Department of Neurology, Bukhara State Medical Institute

Resenzents:

N.A Khodzhaeva – head of the Department of emergency neurology of the Bukhara branch of the scientific center of emergency ambulance of the Republic.

S.N. Rakhmatova is a candidate of Medical Sciences (PhD)., Associate Professor, Department of Neurology, Bukhara State Medical Institute.

Salomova Nilufar Qahhorovna-PhD, assistant Department of Neurology, Bukhara State Medical Institute

More than 30 scientific works have been published in domestic and foreign journals.

The monograph is dedicated to acute circulatory failure of the brain, which is one of the current pressing problems, and now comprehensive measures are being implemented to develop an effective system in the medical field of our country, including the early diagnosis of neurological diseases among different segments of the population and reducing their complications, the timely detection of clinical signs of re-strokes, and

The monograph was the result of many years of research work by the author, and the results obtained showed a special interest in the diagnosis and treatment process.

The monograph was carried out according to the plan of research work of the Bukhara State Medical Institute, named after Abu Ali ibn Sino.

The monograph is intended for neurologists, general practice physicians, clinical interns, and master's students in the specialty of neurology of the Supreme Court of Medicine.

Content:

1.	1. Chapter: Clinical-pathogenetic aspects of recurrent ischemic and hemorrhagic strokes (literature review)	9
	1.1 Epidemiological aspects of recurrent strokes	
	1.2 Risk factors for recurrent strokes	
	1.3 Etiological and pathogenetic aspects of relapsed strokes	
	1.4 Biochemical aspects of recurrent strokes	
	1.5 Clinical aspects of recurrent strokes	
	1.6 Features of treatment and rehabilitation measures in patients with recurrent stroke	
2.	2 Chapter: Clinical features, research materials and methods of primary rehabilitation measures in men and women with recurrent ischemic and hemorrhagic stroke	44
	2.1 Distribution of patients with recurrent stroke by gender, age and type of stroke	
	2.2 Research methods	
	2.2.1 Instrumental research methods	
	2.2.2 Laboratory examination methods	
	2.3 Methods of conducting rehabilitation measures	
	2.4. Ma statistical data processing	

3.	3. Chapter: Clinical and pathogenetic properties of relapsed strokes	73
	3.1. Comparative clinical and pathogenetic features of strokes	
	3.2. Clinical picture of ischemic and hemorrhagic strokes, depending on the pathogenetic subgroup	
	3.3. Features of the clinical course of relapsed ischemic and hemorrhagic strokes in patients who have undergone a stroke, depending on the focus of damage, gender, and age	
	3.4. Practical study of speech and thinking	
4.	4. Chapter: Comparative significance of the results of laboratory and neurovisual examinations in patients with recurrent ischemic and hemorrhagic stroke	114
	4.1. Comparative importance of risk factors for relapsed strokes in patients	
	4.2. Analysis of the results of laboratory tests	
5.	5. Chapter: IOC features of neurorehabilitation itself in the post-relapsed acute disorder of blood circulation in the cranial brain	161
	5.2. Measures for rehabilitation of patients who have had a re-stroke and who have somatic pathology	

6.	Conclusions	185
7.	List of literature	187
8.	List of published scientific works	212
9.	Abbreviations	215

CHAPTER I.
THE LITERATURE REVIEW.

1- Clinical-pathogenetic aspects of recurrent ischemic and hemorrhagic strokes

1.1 Epidemiological aspects of recurrent strokes

Stroke is an acute disorder of cerebral circulation characterized by the onset of sudden (a few minutes, hours) onset, focal or cranial neurological symptoms, lasting more than 24 hours [3,177].

To date, the incidence and mortality of cerebral stroke remain among the highest in the world. Every year, the number of stroke injuries in the country suffers from more than 450,000 people (1 in every 200 inhabitants), 35% of whom die in the acute period of the disease, and 55–80% remain disabled [11, 176]. Basically, patients often die during the acute period of strokes observed in the trunk blood vessels of the brain [12, 169]. The mortality rate increases by 10–15% by the end of the first year after acute circulatory disorders in the brain, and the number of survivors in the acute period for 5 years is about half of the patients. Year after year, there is an increase in the number of strokes in the Republic of Uzbekistan, and this indicator continues to grow, rejuvenating day after day. 80–85% of all strokes are ischemic strokes, with a frequency four times higher than that of a hemorrhagic stroke, equivalent to 4:1.

Transistor ischemic ataxia is an important factor in the development of brain infarction. Patients who have transitory ischemic ataxia have a 4-5% per year risk of developing ischemic stroke [22, 159]. The most dangerous factors for ischemic and hemorrhagic strokes are divided into groups that cannot be changed. Dangerous factors that cannot be changed are age and gender. The risk factors that can be changed, that is, those harmful habits that are common and make up the largest percentage, According to the Ministry of Health, for older people, in 2012, cerebrovascular diseases accounted for about 17% of cases, causing a recurrence of cerebral strokes. Impaired cerebral circulation after Primary Stroke leads to further exacerbation of the symptoms of dissirculatory encephalopathy [29, 151]. As a result of the relapse of the transistor ischemic ataxia, there is an annual increase in the risk of strokes of 14% per year and a constant increase over the next five years. The study found that the risk of stroke complications occurring after acute circulatory disorders of the cranium was highest, did not change within three years of Primary Stroke, and then regressed.

In a stroke, brain damage has serious consequences. The mortality rate after relapsing ischemic stroke is two times higher, with 12% to 35% of patients being found to die in the first month after re-stroke [36, 145]. Primary ischemic strokes have a mortality rate of 42%, with re-stroke ending in mortality in 65-70% of patients [49, 141]. In many cases, re-strokes lead to a change in the patient's quality of life and severe disability. Often, they lead to self-service, fading interest in life, becoming incapable of acting as well, and a decrease in the way they live socially. Post-stroke disability ranks first among all causes and occurs in 32 of the 100,000 population [5, 133]. Due to neurological deficits, i.e., movement, intuition, and cognitive impairment, the patient loses a number of spiritual, social, and mental skills, which leads to a decrease in social activity and quality of life [18, 130]. Thus, relapsed strokes in male and female patients are considered an urgent medical and social problem.

1.2 Risk factors for recurrent strokes

The risk factor is a sign that precedes the disease, has an independent, stable probability relationship, and is important in predicting it. The risk factor is a predictive factor that allows you to predict the likelihood of the occurrence of the disease individually and in general in the population. Timely identification and prevention of risk factors is a promising direction to prevent acute disruption of cerebral circulation. According to the WHO (2013), about 300 risk factors for stroke have been described, but factors that occur at high frequencies in different populations have a significant impact on the development of the pathological condition and reduce the incidence of its prevention. The co-occurrence of several risk factors increases the likelihood of stroke origin (according to Who (2013), if there are 1-2 factors, the risk of stroke is 6%, and if there are 3 factors and more, it is 19%). Risk factors are divided into types that cannot be conditionally modified and those that can be modified. Age, gender, heredity, ethnicity, and geographical factors are among the factors that cannot be changed. Factors that can be changed include diseases resulting from harmful habits (tobacco smoking, drug use, excessive alcohol consumption, obesity, anemia, depression, psychoemotional stress, having a more sedentary life, and having less reactivity) and underlying diseases [26, 144]. Major diseases that cause recurrent cranial stroke include arterial hypertension, heart disease, diabetes mellitus, atherosclerosis of the carotid arteries, and dyslipidemia [28, 98]. Elderly patients usually have several risk factors that include metabolic changes and comorbidities. Arterial hypertension is one of the most dangerous factors that provokes the development of stroke. Arterial hypertension is characterized by metabolic changes, changes in the vascular wall, and, in particular, hemodynamic changes in the system and brain. This, in turn, is a dangerous factor that leads not only to the origin of re-hemorrhagic stroke but also to re-ischemic stroke. The prevalence of arterial hypertension in the Russian Federation is 39.2% among men and 41.1% among women. 37.1% of men and 58.9% of women know about their diseases, and of these (often not effective enough), 21.6% of men and 46.7% of women carry out treatment measures. According to the 2013 territorial population census, arterial hypertension is recorded in 89.2% of patients with acute circulatory disorders in the brain in Russia.

Diastolic arterial blood pressure is 105 mm.sim.who. the risk of developing a stroke when it is equal to diastolic arterial blood pressure of 76 mm.sim.who. 10 times higher than the equivalent. Thus, patients with primary cranial stroke belong to a very high-risk group, requiring normalization of blood pressure and careful selection of antihypertensive drugs [34, 99]. However, a number of studies show that the ratio of patients with arterial hypertension with primary and recurrent strokes is approximately the same [43.96].

Cardiovascular disease is the causative agent of cardioembolic ischemic stroke and is also one of the leading causes of hemodynamic strokes. In angioneurological practice, current research methods such as Holter monitoring and transthoracic transesophageal exocardiography have made it possible to expand the list of heart diseases that cause brain injuries [46, 92]. Nevertheless, in the first place, compartment fibrillation (swinging arrhythmia) causes the origin of the cardioembolic subtype of ischemic stroke. Swinging arrhythmia increases the risk of developing a stroke by five times and increases the mortality rate from this disease by 1.58 times. According to Fremingham studies, swinging arrhythmias were reported in 1.5% of patients in the 50–59 age group and in the 80–89 age group in 23.5% of cases [33.91]. Swinging arrhythmia is an independent risk factor leading to re-stroke and death among patients who had a primary stroke a month earlier [63, 89]. In old age, sinoatrial node fibrosis and fatty infiltration are two of the causes of an increase in the frequency of compartment fibrillation.

In addition to cardiac arrhythmias, the cause of cardiogenic embolism can also be other heart diseases that contribute to the formation of thrombosis in the cavity. For patients with acute myocardial infarction and post-infarction cardiac aneurysms, heart valve prostheses are also considered a potential risk factor for cranial inultation. Hypercholesterolemia and lipid metabolism disorders (reduction of high-density lipoproteins, increase of low-density lipoproteins, hypertriglyceridemia) are characterized by the development of atherosclerosis, ranking alongside arterial hypertension, which is the main cause of the development of cerebral stroke [81, 93]. In the elderly, there is an increase in cholesterol in diseases accompanied by metabolic disorders; it is for this reason that the increase in its amount does not depend on age. The risk of developing the atherothrombotic subspecies of ischemic stroke is inextricably linked with cranial artery stenosis and occlusion levels. With a sleep artery stenosis rate of more than 75%, the annual risk of transistor ischemic ataxia is 13%, while stroke is 3% and carotid stenosis is 70–99%. Then the risk of developing a stroke is 5–7% per year. With age, several cranial trunk blood vessels undergo occlusive atherosclerotic damage; that is, the frequency of occurrence of the process of atherogenesis goes back. The fact that damage to multiple cranial vessels occurs two times more than damage to one trunk vascular vessel occurs mainly among patients over 65 years of age [94.95].

Another of the independent risk factors for the development of ischemic stroke is diabetes mellitus. Most often, diabetes mellitus is not diagnosed in elderly patients with cerebral stroke, although it can occur in 50% of patients. Stroke is usually severe in patients with diabetes mellitus, with impaired carbohydrate metabolism characterized by high mortality and disability [82, 111]. According to clinical data, the frequency of ischemic stroke in patients with diabetes compared to blood clots is 5–6 times greater [83, 112]. In most patients with diabetes mellitus who experience ischemic types of acute circulatory disorders in the brain, stroke does not have thrombotic properties, in the development of which a slowdown in oxidative processes, damage to the sympathetic vasomotor nerves, and chronic cranial vascular failure, which causes hypocapnia, occupy a leading position. The causes of the development of ischemic thrombotic stroke in patients with diabetes mellitus are significant atherosclerotic changes in the blood vessels of the brain, an increase in blood viscosity, and a violation of its coagulation properties (inhibition of the anti-coagulation system and activation of coagulation systems). The occurrence of depression was found to be directly related to the duration of diabetes mellitus in patients, damage to the vascular system, and protective resistive processes. Damage to the cranial arteries (carotid and spinal arteries) plays an important role in the development of cerebrovascular disease, which is more associated with atherosclerosis in diabetes [84, 118].

The information that excessive alcohol consumption leads to the development of a cerebral stroke has been the cause of various disagreements to this day. Alcohol-induced arterial hypertension, parasympathetic cardiac denervation, hypercoagulant conditions, decreased cerebral blood flow, and ulcerative fibrillation lead to an increased risk of stroke origin [101, 120]. In addition, regular alcohol consumption is considered to be responsible for the origin of toxic encephalopathy. In all patients, etiological causes, the problem of alcoholism, and risk factors have not yet been sufficiently studied. At the same time, 5.4–10% of all patients admitted to a psychiatric hospital diagnosed with alcoholism are over the age of 60 [102, 121]. Often, such patients are not treated by lying in a dispensary. Elderly alcoholism has been reported in patients older than 65 years and ranks third among psychiatric disorders [103, 124]. Another risk factor is smoking, which is also an important risk factor for ischemic strokes. However, there is also some disagreement about this, and the direct effect has not been proven, perhaps because it has a multi-factor character. The effect of tobacco as a risk factor for blood vessels is primarily due to the acceleration of the process of atherogenesis, which leads to the contraction of the muscle layer of the arteries. This, in turn, leads to the appearance of arterial hypertension and atherosclerosis. It has also been found that people who smoke tobacco are at risk of developing type 2 diabetes [134].

Abdominal obesity and hypodynamia are important risk factors for cerebral strokes. A number of studies have shown that there is a direct correlation: the greater the body weight, the higher the risk of developing ischemic stroke. Regular exercise leads to a decrease in body weight, a decrease in blood pressure, a decrease in total cholesterol levels, and, indirectly, a decrease in the risk of stroke. However, no study has proven that weight loss leads to a reduction in the risk of relapsed strokes [136]. The effect of this factor on the appearance of cardiovascular pathology is complex. Risk factors such as arterial hypertension with obesity, diabetes mellitus of the second type, and dyslipidemia are often inextricably linked with each other [140]. The combination of abdominal obesity, dyslipidemia, increased blood pressure, and increased blood glucose levels has been called a metabolic syndrome in the literature. Metabolic syndrome, in a broad sense, is a complex of interconnected endocrine and metabolic disorders that increase the risk of the formation of cardiovascular pathology. The frequency of occurrence of the metabolic syndrome occurs in 14–24% of the population and in 43% of patients with cerebrovascular disease [146]. Each of the pathological conditions is an independent risk factor, but their combined effect increases the risk of developing vascular injuries several times. According to research, this is 42–43.5% among patients over the age of 60, and as patients with metabolic syndrome age, body weight also increases [150]. Knowledge of the characteristics of risk factors for relapsed strokes in all patients makes it possible to correctly reflect the planning of preventive measures. 1.3. Etiological and pathogenetic aspects of relapsed strokes As a result of a re-violation of blood circulation in the brain, the rate of passage of impulses in the central nervous system decreases, which in turn leads to the braking of the entire metabolic process. [110,175]. Every day, the human brain loses 6 million neurons from its 100 billion starting neurons. [114,170]. Changes affect the white matter of the brain, which is manifested by the leukareosis process, which is recorded in a third of patients aged 65 and 84 [117, 171]. Nerve tissue atrophy also causes a number of changes in the cranial blood vessels that cause circulatory disorders in the cranial brain. In patients with recurrent stroke, the elasticity of the arteries decreases, regardless of the development of atherosclerosis. Elastic fibers and smooth muscles can replace collagen. In blood vessels with lost elasticity, this process does not exist. Atherosclerosis of the arteries is an independent risk factor in the development of arterial hypertension and vascular diseases. Metabolic regulation of capillary blood vessels, decreased elasticity, and increased resistance of arteries lead to a decrease in the antiagregation properties of the walls of blood vessels. These ravines, in turn caused by an age-related increase in the hypercoagulation activity of the blood, contribute to the emergence of chronic cranial ischemia [19, 131].

In ischemic stroke, occlusion of a cranial blood vessel or a violation or decrease in blood circulation in the cranial brain within a few minutes leads to a deterioration in blood supply to the cranial brain and the death of neurons in the central ischemic area. Ischemic necrosis, called the ischemic area or penumbra area, involves the competent areas of vital organs that are functionally affected in the environment but are supplied with blood from the collateral vessels at the same time. This part of the brain tissue can become the ischemic area, that is, the area of necrosis, since secondary damage to neurons caused by a cascade of entire hemodynamic cells and metabolic ravines leads to the gradual loss of cranial cells over several days from the moment of cerebral artery occlusion [40, 126]. Despite the fact that the ischemic cascade is as versatile as it seems, it is individual in each individual case. Age-related changes in the central nervous system described above are reflected in the formation of the Ischemia Center. It is known that cerebral ischemic strokes are heterogeneous in line with the modern pathogenetic classification [42, 132]. In stroke status, the ratio of pathogenetic subtypes is individual for each age group [47, 135]. Today, in most economically developed countries, atherosclerotic lesions of the main arteries of the head are most common in patients, which are diagnosed in 94% of cases. Very small changes in blood pressure in people with deep stenosis of several main vessels of the brain can lead to the appearance or exacerbation of focal cranial symptoms, and a decrease in blood pressure with a weakening of cardiac activity can be a direct cause of death. The prevalence of atherothrombotic strokes is almost the same in patients of all ages. In about 50% of ischemic strokes, pathological changes were found in the extracranial arteries [59, 137]. In patients with many years of hypertension, symptoms of leukoreosis at MCKT and lacunar strokes are very common. Hypertonic angiopathy affects small-diameter arteries feeding subcortical white matter [60, 138]. The high prevalence of heart disease in patients with circulatory disorders in the brain increases the risk of cardioembolic and hemodynamic stroke. It often causes fibrillation of the heart cavity due to embolism in patients with post-infarction cardiosclerosis. The risk of stroke is 5 times higher in patients with ulcerative fibrillation and arrhythmias with vascular permeability of the heart and 10 times higher in patients with chronic heart failure [7, 64]. Decreased blood conduction function of the myocardium in patients with ulcerative fibrillation and arrhythmias can lead to worsening blood flow in the brain and cause the development of recurrent strokes [14, 68]. Congenital heart defects, mitral clapn prolapse, and rheumatism often present at a young age, and this leads to the formation of small or medium ischemia foci, setting the stage for the appearance of cardioembolism [16, 69]. In ischemic stroke, occlusion of a cranial blood vessel or a violation or decrease in blood circulation in the cranial brain within a few minutes leads to a deterioration in blood supply to the cranial brain and the death of neurons in the central ischemic area. Ischemic necrosis, called the ischemic area or penumbra area, involves the competent areas of vital organs that are functionally affected in the environment but are supplied with blood from the collateral vessels at the same time. This part of the brain tissue can become the ischemic area, that is, the area of necrosis, since secondary damage to neurons caused by a cascade of entire hemodynamic cells and metabolic ravines leads to the gradual loss of cranial cells over several days from the moment of cerebral artery occlusion [40, 126]. Despite the fact that the ischemic cascade is as versatile as it seems, it is individual in each individual case. Age-related changes in the central nervous system described above are reflected in the formation of the Ischemia Center. It is known that cerebral ischemic strokes are heterogeneous in line with the modern pathogenetic classification [42, 132]. In stroke status, the ratio of pathogenetic subtypes is different for each age group [47, 135]. Today, in most economically developed countries, atherosclerotic lesions of the main arteries of the head are most common in patients and are diagnosed in 94% of cases. Very small changes in blood pressure in people with deep stenosis of several main vessels of the brain can lead to the appearance or exacerbation of focal cranial symptoms, and a decrease in blood pressure with a weakening of cardiac activity can be a direct cause of death. The prevalence of atherothrombotic strokes is almost the same in patients of all ages. In about 50% of ischemic strokes, pathological changes were found in the extracranial arteries [59, 137]. In patients with many years of hypertension, symptoms of leukoreosis at MSKT and lacunar strokes are very common. Hypertonic angiopathy affects small-diameter arteries feeding subcortical white matter [60, 138]. The high prevalence of heart disease in patients with circulatory disorders in the brain increases the risk of cardioembolic and hemodynamic stroke. It often causes fibrillation of the heart cavity due to embolism in patients with post-infarction cardiosclerosis. The risk of stroke is 5 times higher in patients with ulcerative fibrillation and arrhythmias with vascular permeability of the heart and 10 times higher in patients with chronic heart failure [7, 64]. Decreased blood conduction function of the myocardium in patients with ulcerative fibrillation and arrhythmias can lead to worsening blood flow in the brain and cause the development of recurrent strokes [14, 68]. Congenital heart defects, mitral clapn prolapse, and rheumatism often present at a young age, and this leads to the formation of small or medium ischemia foci, setting the stage for the appearance of cardioembolism [16, 69]. In ischemic stroke, occlusion of a cranial blood vessel or a violation or decrease in blood circulation in the cranial brain within a few minutes leads to a deterioration in blood supply to the cranial brain and the death of neurons in the central ischemic area. Ischemic necrosis, called the ischemic area or penumbra area, involves the competent areas of vital organs that are functionally affected in the environment but are supplied with blood from the collateral vessels at the same time. This part of the brain tissue can become the ischemic area, that is, the area of necrosis, since secondary damage to neurons caused by a cascade of entire hemodynamic cells and metabolic ravines leads to the gradual loss of cranial cells over several days from the moment of cerebral artery occlusion [40, 126]. Despite the fact that the ischemic cascade is as versatile as it seems, it is individual in each individual case. Age-related changes in the central nervous system described above are reflected in the formation of the Ischemia Center. It is known that cerebral ischemic strokes are heterogeneous in line with the modern pathogenetic classification [42, 132]. In stroke status, the ratio of pathogenetic subtypes is different for each age group [47, 135]. Today, in most economically developed countries, atherosclerotic lesions of the main arteries of the head are most common in patients and are diagnosed in 94% of cases. Very small changes in blood pressure in people with deep stenosis of several main vessels of the brain can lead to the appearance or exacerbation of focal cranial symptoms, and a decrease in blood pressure with a weakening of cardiac activity can be a direct cause of death. The prevalence of atherothrombotic strokes is almost the same in patients of all ages. In about 50% of ischemic strokes, pathological changes were found in the extracranial arteries [59, 137]. In patients with many years of hypertension, symptoms of leukoreosis at MSKT and lacunar strokes are very common. Hypertonic angiopathy affects small-diameter arteries feeding subcortical white matter [60, 138]. The high prevalence of heart disease in patients with circulatory disorders in the brain increases the risk of cardioembolic and hemodynamic stroke. It often causes fibrillation of the heart cavity due to embolism in patients with post-infarction cardiosclerosis. The risk of stroke is 5 times higher in patients with ulcerative fibrillation and arrhythmias with vascular permeability of the heart and 10 times higher in patients with chronic heart failure [7, 64]. Decreased blood conduction function of the myocardium in patients with ulcerative fibrillation and arrhythmias can lead to worsening blood flow in the brain and cause the development of recurrent strokes [14, 68]. Congenital heart defects, mitral clapn prolapse, and rheumatism often present at a young age, and this leads to the formation of small or medium ischemia foci, setting the stage for the appearance of cardioembolism [16, 69]. A violation of hemodynamics can lead to a violation of the functioning of the heart and the development of cardiac hypodynamic syndrome. Thus, a violation of the rhythm leads to a decrease in the volume of work of the left ventricle and, in turn, a decrease in blood pressure and the complete supply of blood vessels in the cerebral hemispheres. Modified vessels, in turn, do not have sufficient reactivity to fully maintain adequate cerebral perfusion; this causes the development of hemodynamic stroke, which is very rare at the age of 65 [24, 70].

Ischemic strokes occur in patients at night or early in the morning [27, 72]. Degenerative-dystrophic lesions of the cervical region of the spinal cord occur in 10% of people over 50, 17% of people over 60, and 43% of people over 70 [52.73]. Exposure to arteries in the vertebro-basal basin is associated with osteochondrosis, disc hernia, deformity of the spinal canal, and, against the background of trauma to the cervical spine, the appearance of osteophytes in unco vertebral arthrosis. Today, the issues of etiopathogenesis and pathogenetics between primary and recurrent strokes have not been sufficiently studied. Concomitant damage to the cerebral arteries, anatomical defects, and vascular anomalies cause re-stroke in patients. Decreased cerebral internal blood flow, insufficient performance of blood flow in the collateral blood vessel's own function, and decreased reactivity of cranial blood vessels are the impetus for stroke development and progression [53, 74]. An objective assessment of the importance of extra- and intravasal effects in the occurrence of cerebral circulation disorders should be carried out by correlating the manifestations of clinical signs in patients, laboratory results, and research conclusions with indicators of instrumental examination [58]. Another common cause of re-strokes in patients is embolism of the heart or cholesterol [61, 75]. Recurrent hemorrhagic strokes are not sufficiently noted in patients to date, the cause of which is hypertension; aneurysms and vascular malformations are considered and often manifest up to 60 years of age. In addition, amyloid accumulation in small-diameter arteries in Adventism is manifested by the occurrence of amyloid angiopathy. In patients over 60 years of age with hemorrhagic stroke, this morphological finding occurs in 8% of cases, and in patients over 90 years of age, it occurs in more than 60% of cases. The formation of fibrinoid necrosis and microaneurysms in the arteriole wall is associated with amyloid accumulation [67, 76].

1.4. Biochemical aspects of recurrent strokes

In brain injuries, biochemical mechanisms include impaired oxygen supply to neurons as a result of acute ischemia, which in turn causes pathological-neurological reactions; that is, as a result of insufficient glucose and oxygen reaching the brain tissue, anaerobic glycolysis is activated, as a result of which lactic acid begins to accumulate inside the cell, and the work of potassium ion channels is The transfer of Ca and Na ions to neurons increases, and the periodic oxidation process of lipids is activated. While Na ions are responsible for intracellular transfer and the high accumulation of water in it, the large transfer of Ca ions has a catastrophic effect on enzymatic processes. As a result of this, cytotoxic substances appear and, increasingly, neuronal destruction intensifies. Some of the reactions that appear later in the acute period play an important role; along with them, phenomena such as endothelial dysfunction, anticoagulant potential of the vessel wall, and progressive metabolic disorders are summarized [31, 77]. The characteristics of the biochemical cascade in patients with re-stroke are assessed along with the premorbid state of the body, the nature of metabolic processes, and many other factors [54, 78]. Age-related changes in the hormonal background also have a dangerous effect on the development of stroke. In women of reproductive age, the cranium is less susceptible to vascular pathology due to the protective effects of estrogens, which reduce the spread of smooth myocytes and normalize lipid metabolism. In menopause, the antiaterogenic effects of hormones go away. In addition, neuroendocrine imbalance develops because hypersympathicotonia causes norepinephrine to increase blood circulation, which is one of the causes of arterial hypertension [8, 79]. Modern research suggests that the role of inflammation in the development of the ischemic furnace and cranial vascular atherogenesis is important [9, 80]. Inflammatory changes are accompanied by the formation of atherosclerotic plaques, resulting in the migration of monocytes, lymphocytes, and macrophage cells from the vascular wall [37, 166]. Plaque damage and destabilization occur in the presence of macrophages and plasma cells in their composition. In the acute period of strokes, active inflammation leads to an increase in the area of necrotic tissues in the brain [50, 167]. This also applies to ischemic and hemorrhagic strokes. Concomitant diseases and patient conditions (hypertension, diabetes mellitus, and dyslipidemia) affect the activity of cells involved in the inflammatory process. Thus, patients with heart and vascular disease have significantly higher blood plasma concentrations [56, 165]. Cholesterol serves to increase monocyte activity and, according to some authors, can activate endothelial cells [66, 162]. In addition, it has been found to be related to the level of inflammatory proteins, markers, and burn diseases listed above (fibrinogen, C-reactive protein). The transition to anti-inflammatory reactions is a characteristic of aging itself, exhibiting age-related changes in the immune system [71, 161]. With age, fno- increases tissue production, while the synthesis of the most important anti-inflammatory marker, il-10, decreases [128, 161].

Meanwhile, stroke involves an in-depth study of metabolism and hemostasis, including the interrelated multilateral processes that occur in the body, in order to understand biochemical processes. Disorders of hemostasis combine with a cascade of biochemical reactions, leading to necrosis of the brain tissue. Hemostasis is constantly changing, directly damaging the brain and altering many of the signals of its molecules' blood centers. In the acute period of strokes, an increase in the activity of blood clotting (fibrinogen, thrombin-antithrombin III, VI, and VIII factors) is observed; the thromboresistance of the vascular wall decreases; the activity of the anticogulant system decreases (the blood center of the C-reactive protein decreases); and fibrinolysis activity decreases [139, 156]. A number of studies have shown that with age, the coagulation index increases and a decrease in blood clotting time is observed. Platelet aggregation is observed to increase by 4% to 20–30 years of age and by 8–10% to 40–50 years of age. Aggregation activity in humans decreases by 7-8% after the age of 50. In the norm, the viscosity of blood increases in women and men under 50 years of age, followed by a decrease in age as a result of physiological anemization of the IOC. Platelet interactions with endothelial cells of atherothrombotic and lacunar subtypes are considered important in the development of cerebral circulation disorders [142, 157]. Patients who have atherosclerosis with the manifestation of symptoms of chronic ischemia of the brain have a significant level of cholesterol and triglycerides, fibrinogen, platelet aggregation, and fibrinolytic activity that is significantly lower than the norm at significant levels. It has been reported that elderly patients are more susceptible to hypercoagulation than younger ones, which is also manifested by decreased fibrinolytic activity of the blood and increased platelet aggregation. All this makes the brain susceptible to recurrent strokes. The absorption of fibrinogen on the surface of erythrocytes leads to the destabilization of their suspension. The ratio of fibrinogen and albumin blood concentrations in blood plasma can be viewed as suspensory stability, as well as albumin being a natural antagonist of fibrinogen and a very potent deagregant [149, 155]. There are two theories regarding the nature of decreased fibrinolytic activity in older adults compared to younger patients: the first is arterial hypertension, which some researchers consider to be prolonged. The second is considered to be a combination of dyslipidemia and diabetes mellitus [152, 178]. It is important to mention the negative effects of hyperglycemia on the course and outcome of a stroke that can occur as a component of the body's stress response and cause vascular damage or increase Type 2 diabetes. An increase in blood glucose levels leads to swelling of the brain, promotes lactacidosis, and causes the death of neurons in the brain. Patients with severe hyperglycemia have significantly more severe stroke withdrawal [2,153]. With prolonged diabetes mellitus, the occurrence of glycolysis of erythrocyte membranes and hemoglobin proteins is observed. This reduces their deformation, causing changes in the rheological properties of the blood [4, 147]. These disorders indicate changes in the form of erythrocytes in patients with diabetes mellitus [13, 148]. In addition, an increase in blood glucose levels is observed in conjunction with an increase in fibrinogen blood concentration, which increases the aggregation of blood elements and plasma viscosity [25]. A decrease in the content of sialic acids, a decrease in the negative charge on the surface of erythrocytes, a change in the lipid floor, and an increase in the level of glycated hemoglobin will be the reasons for the excessive occurrence of aggregation. Unfortunately, today, the biochemical processes arising after a cranial injury have not been sufficiently studied. The importance of knowledge in this area is invaluable. Having fully studied all the biochemical processes arising after a stroke, we can not only approach the possibilities of treating the affected parts of the brain but also prevent the death of nerve cells.

1.5. Clinical aspects of recurrent strokes

Despite the relevance of the problem of strokes in men and women, the features of the clinical course of patients in this category are still not sufficiently studied. However, there are a number of details that require an individual approach to determining the effectiveness of treatment for men and women

[44, 127]. In men and women, the development of re-strokes is also often caused by conditions such as arterial hypertension, increased blood sugar levels, cardiac arrhythmias, insomnia, impaired blood chemistry, and stress. This in turn reflects changes in the cardiovascular system of the heart, vascular pathologies of the brain, impaired endothelial conduction, and atherosclerotic processes in blood vessels [57, 125]. Re-strokes can often take the form of a syncopated condition. In male and female patients of all ages, ischemic strokes significantly dominate the structure of cerebral vascular pathology. Re-stroke in men and women often develops at night or in the early morning with a decrease in blood pressure and the appearance of atherothrombotic and hemodynamic stroke subtypes. Cardioembolic and lacunar strokes occur during the day when the patient is physically active and strains appear in the body under high pressure as a result of physical exertion and the influence of dangerous factors [23, 122]. Hemorrhagic strokes, which occur in male and female patients aged 65 and older, are observed to be milder in comparison to younger male and female patients. It is severe in young patients and, in many cases, fatal. This may be caused by a number of age-related changes, including dilation of the liquor cavities and failure to obtain complications of occlusive hydrocephalus in time [30, 123]. In the elderly, the volume of bleeding may not be large; it

is limited to parenchyma or ventricles. The spread of blood into the ventricular system can also have a positive effect on the patient's condition, creating the possibility of preventing dislocation syndrome [32, 119]. In male and female patients of old age, recessive neurological deficits are observed. In addition to movement disorders, cognitive disorders occupy the first place in them, which has been reported in only 50% of re-strokes [62, 115]. Cognitive disorders observed in the post-stroke period are most commonly seen in men and women in old age compared to young people, mainly due to low educational quality and the presence of side diseases (diabetes mellitus, hovering arrhythmias, and heart failure [65, 116]. This in turn makes socio-domestic adaptation difficult, even if it is partial, and reduces the effectiveness of rehabilitation measures since, in this category of patients, the degree of inability to treat has a low sensitivity. Their inability to recover and old-age depression reduce the effectiveness of the rehabilitation process. In the acute period of strokes, the mortality rate is observed to rise to a higher level after the age of 75 [85, 113]. This is due to the severity of strokes, frequent cardioembolism, and the presence of side diseases during decompensation. Low-quality medical care is also the cause of this category of patients [87, 108]. Concomitant complications also affect mortality rates. Ischemic stroke complications in patients over 70 years of age account for 62%, and hemorrhagic stroke accounts for 40% [105, 109]. Patients over 65 years of age are three times more susceptible to cranial vascular re-injury after 10 years [106, 173]. Re-stroke is a new cerebrovascular condition that meets one of the following criteria [107, 174]: The occurrence of neurological disorders is different from that of primary stroke; involvement of a new anatomical area or vascular basin; and the occurrence of another pathogenetic subtype distinct from primary stroke are observed. In relapsed stroke, patients are more susceptible to addiction syndrome as they age. The features of the clinical picture of relapsed strokes in patients should be taken into account when drawing up an algorithm of rehabilitation measures.

1.6. Features of treatment and rehabilitation measures in patients with recurrent stroke

Prevention of patients with a re-violation of cerebral circulation should be aimed at preventing the foci of vascular damage, taking into account the causes that lead to stroke. Preventive measures include the methods of medicamentosis and nomedicamentosis. Medicomentosis methods are standard treatment measures and include all types of treatment. Nomedicamentous methods are measures aimed at reconstructing all actions aimed at changing the way of life, that is, speech and cognitive disorders [154]. Recommendations:

abstinence from alcohol and less consumption of table salt are considered to consist of regular exercise and following a healthy lifestyle [158]. Medikamentosis preventive measures include the fight against risk factors such as arterial hypertension and dyslipidemia, filling the hemostasis system with antiagregants, and, when indicated, correction with anticoagulants. In addition, performing surgery on blood vessels in areas with occlusion and stenosis is also one of the preventive measures. Properly selected antihypertensive therapy significantly reduces the incidence and mortality rate of relapsed stroke [160]. In terms of secondary stroke prophylaxis in patients with hemodynamically significant stenosis of extracranial vessels, APF-inhibitors and beta blockers are relatively safe and are recognized as soft-acting drugs that lower blood pressure [164]. Statins are widely used for lipid spectrum correction [168]. Regular consumption of them reduces the likelihood of stroke in patients by 25% [172]. Antiagregants are widely used to normalize the rheological properties of the blood [1]. Anticoagulants are used in pathological disorders of the heart rhythm and valve apparatus. In elderly patients, regular use of antiagregants is recommended because of the high risk of asymptomatic atherosclerosis of the cranial blood vessels and cardiovascular hemodynamic crises [15]. Regular administration of the drug warfarin in all patients with hovering arrhythmias reduces the likelihood of cardioembolic stroke by 68% [38]. In many cases, relapsed strokes lead to a patient's disability and often cause a decrease in self-service ability, making them incapable of eliminating the remaining neurological deficits. Formed neurological deficits, that is, due to movement, intuition, and cognitive disorders, the patient goes on to lose a number of internal and professional skills, which leads to a sharp change in lifestyle. In recent years, neurorehabilitation has been introduced in our country, and rehabilitation technologies have been developed [6]. Recovery can be partially spontaneous, but rehabilitation can help speed up this process and eliminate the remaining neurological deficits, as well as help the patient adapt to new life conditions and preserve neurological deficits. The potential for early rehabilitation is maximal for the first 3 months following cranial vascular injuries [10]. Thus, the initial recovery period of strokes is the most suitable point for directing the patient to the stage of rehabilitation. However, this period determines the need to determine the optimal size of rehabilitation measures and develop adequate rehabilitation programs due to the instability of the situation, the increased somatic pathology that has joined, and the high likelihood of developing complications. [20] Rehabilitation of patients after a stroke involves a number of additional features and difficulties. Relapsed strokes and comorbid conditions reduce the reserve capacity of the heart, neuro-endocrine, and immune systems, which is the age and gender focus of pathogenesis, causing clinical manifestations and complications of strokes. The above defines their importance in the development of rehabilitation programs [21]. The decompensation stage of chronic somatic diseases often significantly limits rehabilitation processes and reduces the likelihood of post-stroke recovery. For example, a sufficient increase in physical activity in patients with burning heart failure can lead to a decrease in physical exercise tolerance, a decrease in the number of contractions of the left ventricular muscles, heart rhythm disorder, and circulatory failure, which in turn can lead to aggravating the post-stroke period or even the appearance of a re-acute violation of cerebral circulation [35]. Nevertheless, the issue of rehabilitation for patients is very relevant. 7% of patients with re-stroke from the first day of cerebral vascular damage and 40–45% a year later are completely dependent on the care of others and cannot move without the help of a person [39]. Care for these patients falls on the shoulders of relatives, medical staff, and social workers. Rehabilitation can be effective due to the processes of nerve tissue regeneration and neurogenesis, the intensity of which depends on the foci of damage and the size of the affected area, as well as the premorbid background [41]. In elderly patients, the potential of neuroplasticity gradually decreases, but ideas about the dynamics of the recovery of the field of motion are controversial. Many researchers deny that the complete restoration of the action function of the lesion furnace depends on age [48]. At the same time, the ability to walk is, in a number of patients, reliably restored more slowly [51]. It is considered a link for elderly patients with cognitive disorders, inertia of mental processes, and the confluence of comorbidity and somatic pathology. During the early rehabilitation recovery period, most patients experience cognitive disorders of varying severity to a certain degree, with post-stroke dementia affecting 5–50% of them. Factors leading to dementia include age, re-strokes in the anamnesis, artificial valves of the heart, axis, arrhythmias, signs of leukorrhea according to neurovisual examinations, and the location of the center in the left hemisphere, among others. Thus, re-violation of cerebral circulation leads to an increased risk of dementia by 5–10 times [17]. According to many researchers, age and gender are considered important in the development of dementia. The reserve capacity of the brain is very wide, allowing it to control chronic degenerative processes without symptoms for a long time. Compensatory mechanisms control auxiliary functions in this case. compensatory mechanisms, the end of their phaolithicity leads to the manifestation of cognitive disorders [45]. Due to changes in the central nervous system, the reserve decreases with age, even if there are no chronic degenerative diseases. So another of the common causes of memory, attention, and intellectual impairment in strokes is Alzheimer's disease. This disease is also considered a risk factor that leads to an exacerbation of symptoms. Physiotherapists, nurses, and speech aphasiologists together recommend that patients with cognitive impairment perform exercises aimed at disease prevention, in a mild form, several times a day, concentrating their minds without exhausting them. Cognitive rehabilitation is carried out taking into account the volume of insufficiency formed under the guidance of a neurologist and neuropsychologist. Patients in this category are not recommended to be prescribed tranquilizers, antidepressants, or sedative drugs. Courses of continuous treatment with vasoactive and nootropic drugs are recommended [55]. A condition that is common for patients with recurrent stroke and further complicates the effectiveness of rehabilitation is post-stroke depression, panic, and astheno-neurotic syndrome. Depression, astheno-neurotic syndrome, fear, and panic cause problems that reduce the objective interpretation of the neurological condition, the quality of life, and the effectiveness of restorative treatment [88]. The reason for the decrease in effectiveness of rehabilitation measures in this case is the disappearance of the patient's confidence in the recovery of the disease, the low level of knowledge, and the absence of the will to find strength for oneself. In addition to antidepressant therapy and psychotherapeutic training, it is accompanied by creating a comfortable atmosphere in the family as well as conducting interviews with close people for early rehabilitation, listening to them, and answering their questions. The initial start of rehabilitation activities helps to form self-service skills, make the patient independent of someone's care, and improve the emotional environment [86]. An important limiting factor in the implementation of a rehabilitation program for patients is somatic pathology, especially the presence of diseases of the cardiovascular system, arrhythmias, and artificial valves. In patients, arterial hypertension, ulcerative fibrillation, stress and tension stenocardia, heart failure, and post-infarction cardiosclerosis come to the fore. In this category of patients, exercise tolerance decreases after the exercise standard, and there are many cases of palpitations, shortness of breath, edema, and orthostatic decrease. Exercise requires the development of individual kinesiotherapy programs with control over their difficulty and tolerance [90]. In the first days, measures are taken to carry out verticalization with monitoring of blood pressure and heart rate. In such patients, physiotherapy measures are recommended to slightly limit Heat treatment (paraffin, ozokerite, clay grease), general baths, hydromassage, and electric laser treatment are strictly prohibited. At all stages of rehabilitation, it is recommended to choose a combination of drugs under the supervision of a cardiologist and take them on time [97]. Age-related features of the musculoskeletal system slow down and limit the effectiveness of rehabilitation. One of the common problems in elderly patients is osteoporosis, which is more likely to increase the risk of fractures in a fall [100]. Degenerative-dystrophic diseases of the spine and deformation from osteoarthritis of the large joints reduce the mobility of patients, which prevents them from activating. For this reason, elderly patients develop arthropathy, muscle atrophy, and bed sores earlier and more frequently. The manifestation of chronic vascular and degenerative diseases of the central nervous system, such as vestibulo-ataxic syndrome, akinetico-rigid syndrome, and age-related vision and hearing disorders, leads to a slowdown in the recovery of walking and self-control abilities. Finally, rehabilitation is adversely affected by social problems (loneliness, social discomfort, financial difficulties) that affect the elderly. Analysis of data from literary sources indicates that elderly patients are most vulnerable to circulatory disorders in the acute brain. This is manifested not only by age-related changes in the vessels of the brain but also by a number of chronic diseases. A decrease in the compression reserve leads to serious consequences of acute circulatory disorders in the brain in this category of patients, and rehabilitation treatments are observed to be limited due to somatic pathology. In the scientific literature, risk factors for the prevention of relapsed strokes are characteristic of elderly patients. Early rehabilitation strategies for patients with circulatory disorders in the cranial brain have not been adequately highlighted. All this emphasizes the need to study the risk factors for re-stroke in patients and then develop a preventive and rehabilitation system.

CHAPTER II.

Clinical features, research materials and methods of primary rehabilitation measures in men and women with recurrent ischemic and hemorrhagic stroke

2.1. Distribution of patients with recurrent stroke by gender, age and type of stroke

The study includes 177 patients with stroke. All patients were brought to the hospital on the first day after the onset of the disease. 137 patients with re-acute circulatory disorders in the brain over a period of 5 years form the main group. The control group was made up of 40 patients who had suffered only one stroke over a period of 5 years. Patient monitoring is carried out in the Department of Neurology. The necessary research is carried out in the Department of Neurology. Comprehensive clinical-neurological examinations of all patients, including careful collection and analysis of complaints by patients, together consist of the collection of somatic pathology and objective and neurological anamnesis. For the study of a neurological patient, examinations are carried out according to the standard scheme.

The National Institutes of Health Stroke Scale (), an activity in daily life rated with the Bartel index, is assessed using the intellectual-cognitive impairment PSASS scale (Mipi-mental State Examination) on hospital admission day and after rehabilitation. The adjacent somatic contractions are determined by the patient and the patient's loved ones on the basis of a survey and with the help of outpatient cards and are diagnosed as follows: Arterial hypertension has a constant blood pressure of 140/90 mmHg, which is determined by the rise in Cardiac dysrhythmias, myocardial ischemia, and scarring changes are recorded during electrocardiography (ECG), with exocardiography (Exocg) practice in necessary halates. Cardiologist doctors are involved in determining the symptoms of chronic heart failure and the degree of clinical withdrawal severity.

During the acute period of their strokes, it is considered necessary for all patients to receive basic non-selective therapy according to the standard for treating strokes, which includes antihypertensive drugs, which improve the rheological properties of the blood.

The main focus of differential treatment should be neuroprotective therapy, which includes nootropic drugs, neuroprotectors, antioxidants, neurotrophic drugs, and regulatory peptides. Male patients with relapsed ischemic stroke were 2 between the ages of 18 and 44 (1.4%), patients aged 45–59 were 35 (52.5%), those aged 60–74 were 28 (41.7%), and patients aged 75–90 were 4 (4.4%). There was no incidence in women between the ages of 18 and 44; patients aged 45–59 were 23 (56.3%); those aged 60–74 were 17 (41.3%); and 75–90 were 4 patients (2.4%) found to be significantly more observable for ischemic stroke in men aged 45–59.

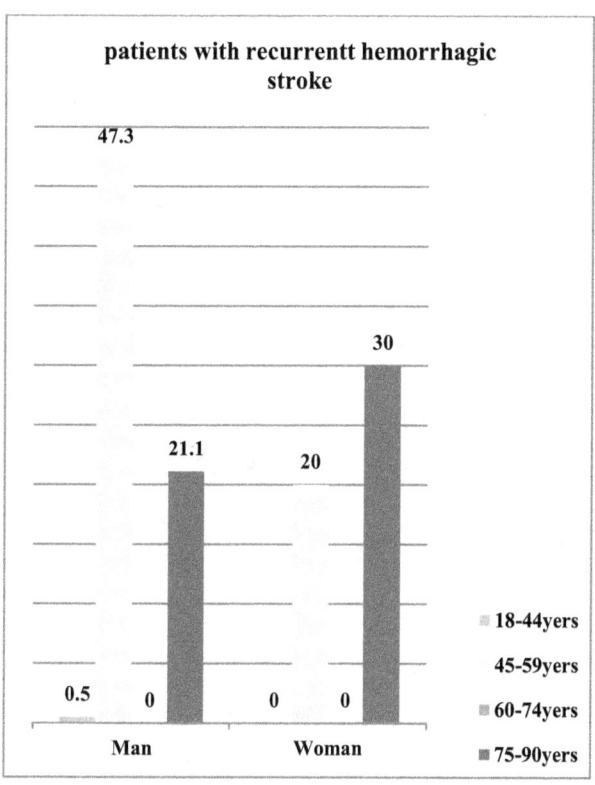

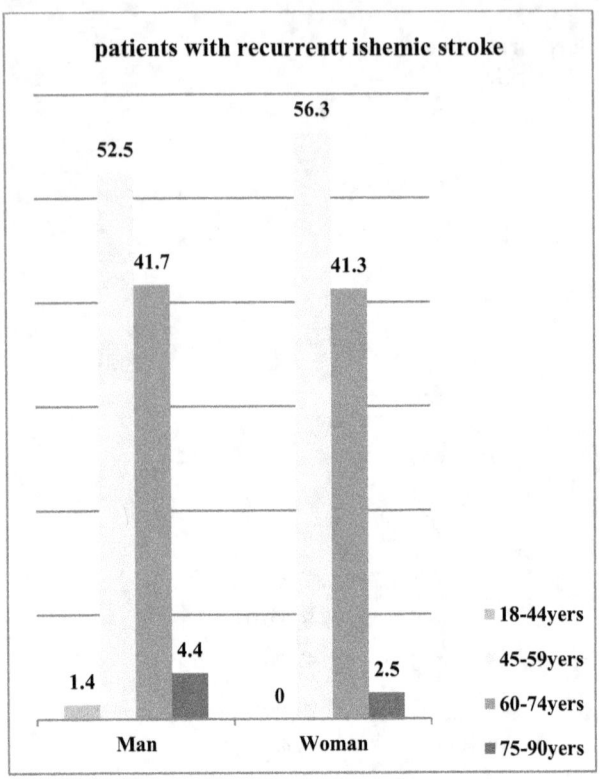

Figure 2.1. Patients with recurrent stroke in the main group distribution by gender and age(n= 137)

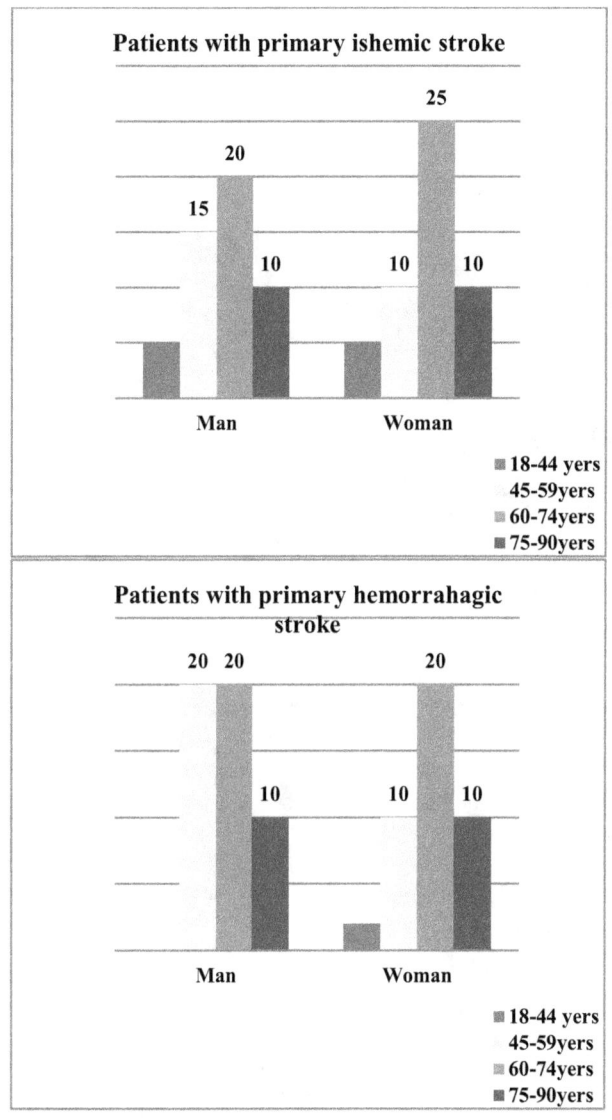

Figure 2.2. Distribution by sex and age of patients with primary hemorrhagic and ischemic stroke in the control group(in%)

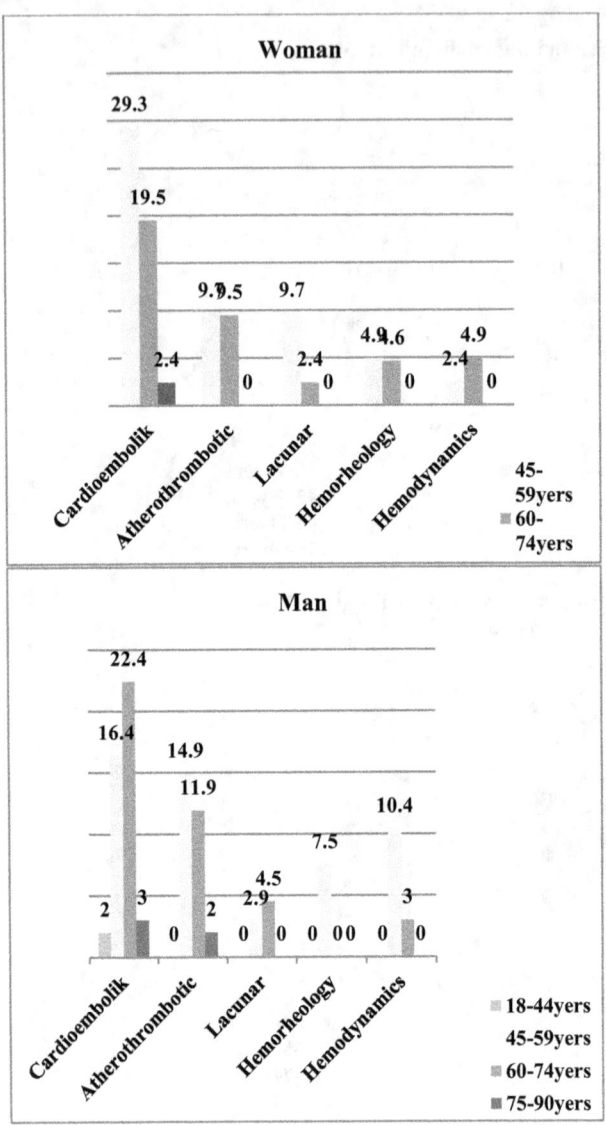

Figure 2.3. Distribution of patients with recurrent ischemic stroke by age, sex, as well as a subtype of stroke

Cardioembolic subtypes have been shown to occur frequently among all subtypes of ischemic stroke in patients of all ages.

Patients were confirmed by the frequent occurrence of relapsed cardioembolic strokes. (Rosamond W., 2018). The second place is occupied by the frequency of atherothrombotic strokes. In addition, the very frequent occurrence of stroke in the core group of the lacunar subtype has been noted. Only men aged 70–75 have been diagnosed with hemorrhagic and hemodynamic strokes.

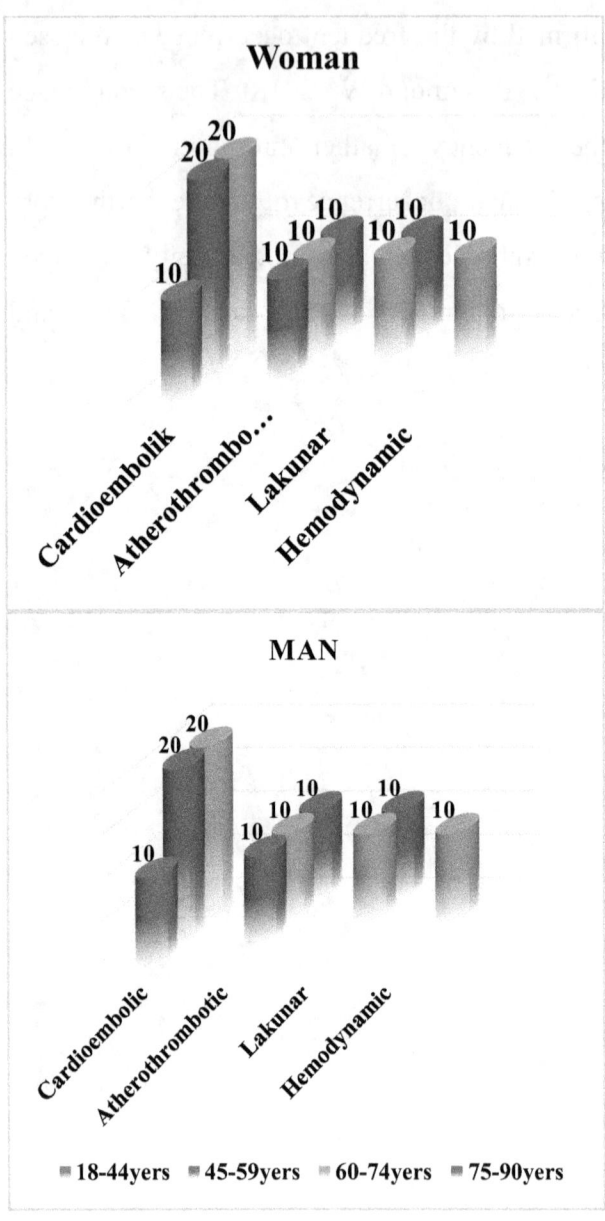

Figure 2.4. Distribution of patients with primary ischemic stroke by age, sex, and subtype of stroke

From the data given, the control group was dominated by the incidence of the atherotrombotic subspecies of stroke among all patients with primary ischemic stroke. The frequency of occurrence of cardioembolic strokes appeared in second place. In 12 (86.2%) of elderly patients with recurrent hemorrhagic stroke, the cause of its origin was arterial hypertension, with 2 (6.9%) AVM, which was found to be 2 (6.9%) ruptured aneurysms and 1 (6.25%) rare factors. As can be seen from Table 2.1, the main cause of recurrent hemorrhagic strokes is arterial hypertension. The causes of strokes at an early age are arteriovenous malformations or ruptured aneurysms.

Table 2.1

Distribution of patients with recurrent hemorrhagic stroke by age, gender, and subtype of stroke

Etiology	18-44 years		45-59 years		60-74 years		75-90 years		all patients
	M	W	M	W	M	W	M	W	
AH	2	2	4	2	5	5	3	2	25
AVM	0	0	1	1	0	0	0	0	2
RA	0	0	1	1	0	0	0	0	2
Total	2	2	6	4	5	5	3	2	29

Note: AH-arterial hypertension, AM-arteriovenous malformations, Yoa-ruptured aneurysm, Kuo-rare factors, M-men; W-women

When detected according to the vascular basin of relapsed strokes, 47 (45.2%) observations observed that the strokes were in the left midbrain basin, 31 (30%) in the right midbrain basin, 24 (23%) in the vertebral basilar basin, 1 (0.9%) in the right forebrain artery basin, and 1 (0.9%) in the left forebrain artery basin (table 2.2).

Table 2.2

Distribution of patients with primary hemorrhagic stroke by age, gender and subtype of stroke

Etiology	18-44 years		45-59 years		60-74 years		75-90 years		all patients
	M	W	M	W	M	W	M	W	
AH	1	1	2	1	2	2	1	1	12
AVM	0	0	1	1	1	1	0	0	4
RA	0	0	1	1	1	1	0	0	4
Total	1	1	4	3	4	4	1	1	20

Note: AH- arterial hypertension, AM- arteriovenous malformations, RA-ruptured aneurysm, RF-rare factors, M-men; W-women

As can be seen from Table 2.2, arterial hypertension is also the main cause of primary hemorrhagic strokes in patients aged 45–59 and 60–74 years. In the control group, the frequency of occurrence according to the vascular basin of patients with primary ischemic stroke is determined as follows: in 11 (35.2%), in the left midbrain artery basin; in 16 (51.6%) of patients, in the right midbrain artery basin; and in 4 (13.2%), in the vertebral artery basin (table 2.3).

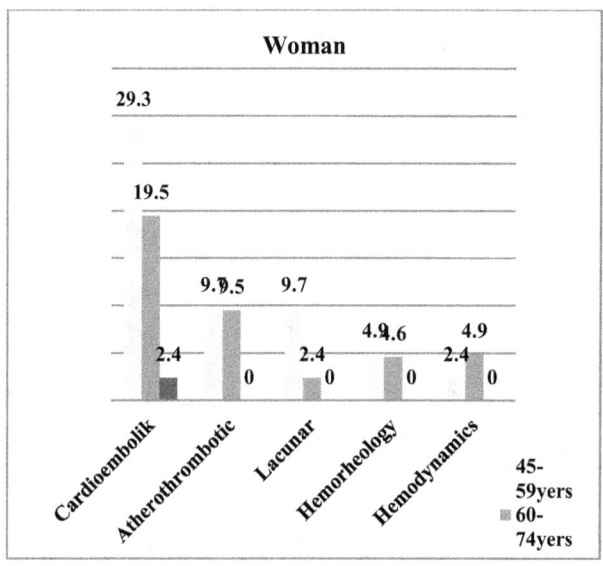

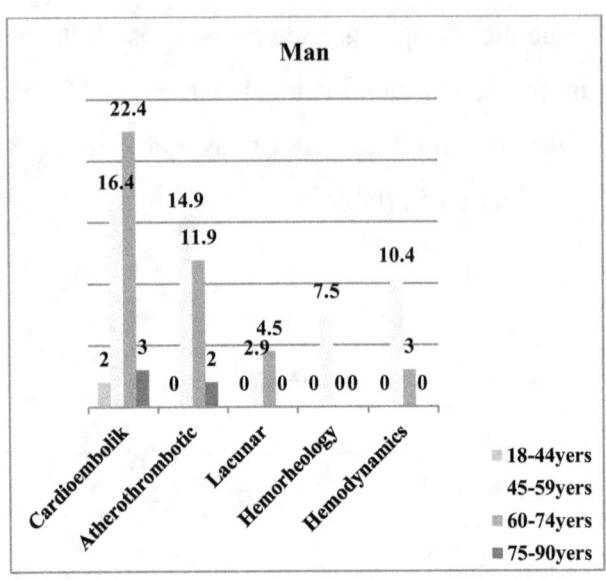

Note: M - men, W -women, LMABB-left middle artery basin of the brain, RMABB-right middle artery basin of the brain, VBB-vertebra-basilar Basin, LAABB-left anterior artery Basin of the brain, RAABB-right anterior artery Basin of the brain

Figure 2.5. Distribution of patients with recurrent ischemic stroke by gender, vascular asin and age

MAN

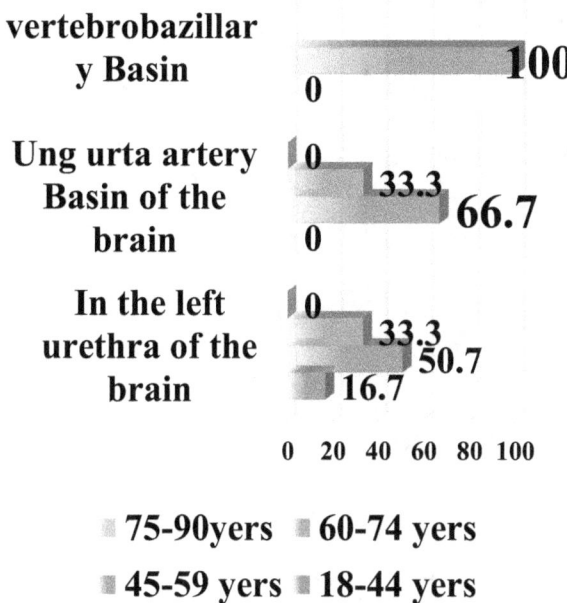

- 75-90yers
- 60-74 yers
- 45-59 yers
- 18-44 yers

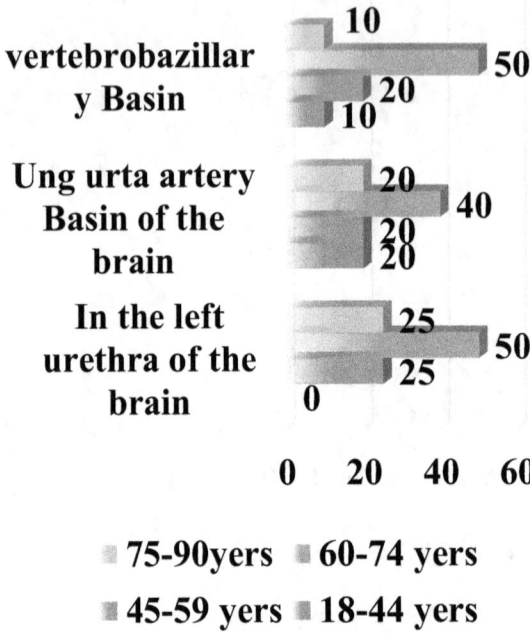

Note: M-men, W-women, LMABB-left middle artery Basin of the brain, RMABB-right middle artery Basin of the brain VBB -vertebra-basilar Basin

Figure 2.6. Distribution of patients with primary ischemic stroke by gender, vascular basin and age

In this analysis of figures 2.5 and 2.6, it is seen that the main and control groups had a higher incidence of strokes in the left midbrain artery basin of the cranium. Recurrent hemorrhagic strokes have 14 (48.2%) subcortical clots, 6 (21.1%) thalamic, 2

(6.7%) putaminal, 3 (10.3%) subarachnoidal, and 4 (13.7%) cerebral clots (table 2.5).

MAN

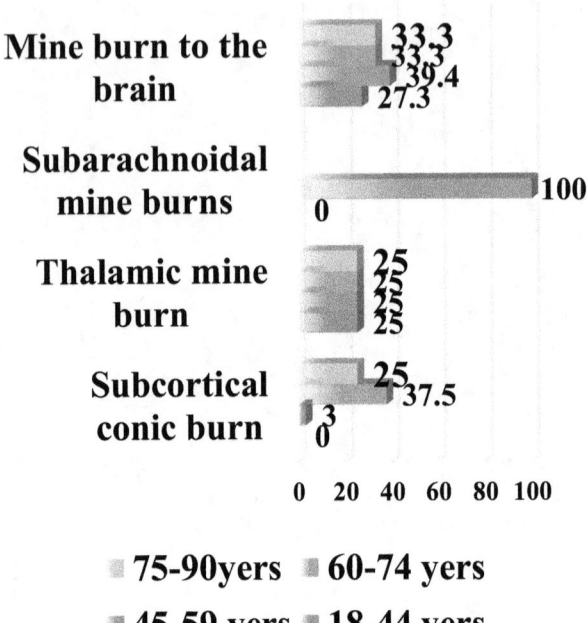

- 75-90yers
- 60-74 yers
- 45-59 yers
- 18-44 yers

WOMAN

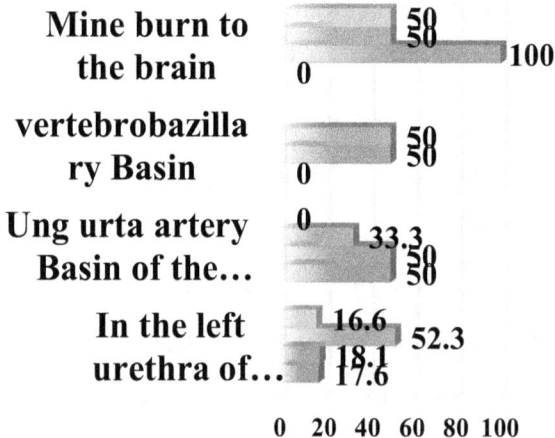

■ 75-90yers ■ 60-74 yers
■ 45-59 yers ■ 18-44 yers

Note: SBT-subcortical blood transfusions, TBT-thalamic blood transfusions, PBT-putamenal blood transfusions, SBT-subarachnoidal blood transfusions, BT-brain transfusion, M-men, W-women

Figure 2.7. Distribution of patients with recurrent hemorrhagic stroke according to gender, age, and blood transfusion localization

In patients in the control group with primary hemorrhagic stroke, when tested for transfusion localization, putaminal clots accounted for 24%, subcortical clots accounted for 14%, and thalamic clots accounted for 6%. According to anamnesis collected from patients with circulatory disorders in the brain, more than 16 patients for 1 year, 40 patients for a duration of 1 to 3 years, and 64 patients for a period of 3 to 5 years were found to suffer. Of these, 29 patients were selected. The average development period for a relapsed ischemic stroke in the main group was 3.67 1.39 years, while hemorrhagic was 4.44 0.73 years. Significant changes were noted in the core group, corresponding to gross neurological deficits. In patients with acute circulatory disorders in the recurrent cranial brain, a serious neurological impairment is most likely associated with the concentration of newly emerging background changes.

2.2. Research methods

The Bartel index covers 10 elements related to self-service and mobility. The level of daily activity is assessed by the sum of the scores determined by the patient for each section of the test. Most items have an assessment grade of "0" (failure to complete the task), "5" (task assistance required), and "10" (complete independence in the task); two items have an assessment grade of "0" (task impossible, or assistance required) and "5" (total independence); and finally, two items have an estimate grade of "0" (total dependence), "5" or "10" (total independence) for situations where assistance is needed. The total count varies from 0 to 100. With such an assessment system, the total score from 0 to 20 corresponds to the full dependence of the patient, from 21 to 60, expressed dependence, from 61 to 90, and from 91 to 99, moderate and mild dependence. (Appendix 2).

PSASS scale. To briefly assess the level of cognitive dysfunction, a "battery of tests for assessing frontal dysfunction" was used, including tasks for conceptual, speech fluency, dynamic Praxis, simple and complex selection reactions, and reflex learning. The total test score is calculated by summing the results for each task. The lower the test result, the more likely the neurological defect will be exactly naioyon. When evaluating the results, the following system was used: A total score of 16–18 corresponds to normal functions or mild cognitive dysfunction; a score of 12–15 indicates more moderate forehead dysfunction; a score of 11 and below is characteristic of clear forehead dysfunction. The possibility of concentration was checked on the basis of the results of the above assignment for output from 100 to 7 and the sample "simple conditional reaction of selection with a violation of the stereotype."

The Trail Makipd test (TMT A and V) is a neuropsychological test of visual attention and attention assessment. It consists of two parts, in which the subject is asked to connect a set of 25 points as quickly as possible while maintaining accuracy. The test can provide information about visual search speed, scanning speed, processing speed, mental agility, and execution functions. Sensitivity is important in detecting dementia-related cognitive impairments, such as Alzheimer's disease. The test is considered one of the most important parts of clinical neuropsychology. The test was created by American neuropsychologist Ralph Reitan. The test was used to evaluate general intelligence in 1944 and is part of the individual general ability exam. In the 1950s, researchers began using a test to assess cognitive dysfunction associated with brain damage, and since then, this test has been used in medicine. Currently, TMT is widely used as a diagnostic tool in a clinical setting. It is known that poor performance is associated with many types of brain diseases, in particular damage to the frontal forehead area. The task requires the subject to connect a sequence of 25 consecutive numbers, similar to the children's puzzle "connecting points" on a sheet of paper or on a computer screen. The test consists of two parts: in the first, the targets must connect all numbers from 1 to 25 in sequential order; in the second part, the points are from 1 to 13 and contain letters from A to L. As in the first part, the patient must combine dots with consecutive letters and numbers, as in 1-a-2-B. 3rd C., in the shortest possible time without lifting the pen off the paper. If an error is made, the test administrator will fix it before moving on to the next item. The purpose of the test is for the test taker to complete both parts as quickly as possible, and the time required to complete the test is used as the main measure of performance. Paper and pencil versions of the test do not record error indicators, but if errors are made, it is assumed that this will be reflected at the time of execution. If the patient has made an error, the test person will notify him immediately, and the patient will be allowed to correct the error. These errors affect the assessment if they are within the time required to correct them. The second part of the test, in which the subject alternates between numbers and letters, is used to check executive functions. The first part is used, first of all, to study the speed of cognitive processing. The score is based on the time spent doing the test (e.g., 35 seconds, which gives a score of 35); the lower the score, the better. There are different norms that allow you to compare groups of the same age. Completion time: the entire test usually lasts from 5 to 30 minutes. The average travel time for parts A and B is 29 and 75 seconds, respectively. If the patient is unable to perform Parts A and B within 5 minutes, there is no need to continue testing. The population in which the social population is calculated includes adolescents, adults, and the elderly.

Currently, it is used as a diagnostic tool in clinical settings. It can provide information about visual search speed, processing speed, scanning, executive functions, and mental agility. In addition, it helps identify cognitive disorders associated with dementia.

The U.S. National Institutes of Health Stroke Scale (NIHSS) is a general medicine IOC designed to assess the severity of a patient's condition with a limp and is used by any physician. The NIHSS is the most common and valid scale in the world and is mandatory for stationary inspection and the determination of the severity of the spine. Analysis of the results of this scale by Brottet et al. was interpreted according to its criteria. (7): 0 score: condition satisfactory; 1-4 score: mild stroke; 5-15 score: moderate to severe stroke; 16-20 score: between moderate and severe stroke; 21-42 score: severe stroke. According to the criteria (7), the result of a total of less than 6 points is a slight stroke; 7–12 points is a stroke of moderate weight; more than 14 points is a severe stroke. (Appendix 3).

Speech recognition. Physiological mechanisms of speech activity

Usually the most important of them, regardless of the variety of signs, is the word. Each word acts as information, message, or information and embodies a specific content (e.g., occupation, notebook, rain, etc.).

The main functions of the language are:

a) Language serves as a means of living and a means of transmitting and mastering social experience from generation to generation (generations of parents, teachers, and mentors);

b) Language is manifested as a means or a way of communication, even as a weapon that controls the actions of people (for example, "there will be no objection," "today is a holiday," which consists of exposure and influence);

c) Another important aspect of language is its ability to serve as a weapon of intellectual activity (understanding the essence of the problem situation, planning a solution, execution, and comparison with the goal). A person is able to plan it, regardless of whether it is a practical or mental action, in contrast to the animal world. The main weapon in the search for a tool for such a plan of activities and solving common opinion issues is language. In psychological research, it has been found that the most basic function of language is communication. Speech activity is the process by which a person uses language for the purpose of mastering socio-historical experience, establishing transmission (transmission) or communication to generations, and planning and carrying out his own personal actions. Speech is considered to consist of the activity of providing information, messages, new knowledge, and solving mental tasks. If language is a means of communication (a weapon), speech is exactly the process itself.

The perception of speech can occur on the basis of the laws of simple reflector activity since the stimuli that cause it consist of triggers of the first type of signals (for example, "March" and "Hello"). Human "signals" (signals) from the occurrence and perception of speech (I.P. Pavlov) can use words of the style. This process takes place in the bark of the large hemispheres of the cranium. When a certain part of the cerebral cortex (the posterior part of the folds on the lower side of the forehead of the left hemisphere of the brain) is damaged, patients experience a violation of speech articulation and call it "speech articulation." K. Wernicke tries to prove that the cranial hemispheres are located on the top side of the forehead area with "sensory aphasia." P.K. In the provision of the Anoxin-speech process, both a physiological mechanism of a rather simple elementary "stimulus-reaction" type and special mechanisms with a characteristic and hierarchical structure for the mechanisms of compact programming of the statement of thought with a speech medium for higher forms of speech activity are involved. Speech mechanisms. (H.I.Jinkin). Before outlining an idea using a speech tool, we draw up the basis of this idea through a special code—it is a programming mechanism. It is followed by a group of mechanisms for the transition from planning to the grammatical structure of a sentence. a mechanism that ensures the practical application of the grammatical features of words to memorization. Mechanism of transition from a structure of the same type to a structure of another type The mechanism of spreading the elements of the program into the grammatical structure Mechanisms that ensure the search for a word according to its meaning Mechanisms that program syntagms in terms of movement Mechanisms for the selection of speech sounds and the transition from the movement program to the filling of sounds A mechanism that ensures the implementation of speech. Researcher A.P. Luria examines the aphasia of speech and states that it consists of the following types:

- dynamic aphasia-speech impairment with the help of sentences;

– efferent motor aphasia-grammatical congestion, violation of the sentence;

– afferent motor aphasia-speech articulation disorder;

- semantic aphasia-violation of sentence correlation;

- sensory aphasia is a disorder of the perception of words.

Periods of speech development		
Period 1	From 2 months	Up to 11 months
Period 2	From 11 months	Up to 19 months
Period 3	From 19 months	Up to 3 months

Speech development has the following characteristics:

a) grinding.

b) buzzing(false words).

c) paradigmatic phonetics (1.3 - 1.5 years old) – grandmother, grandmother, sit, sit, sit.

d) situational bop of speech (J.Piaje-situational speech).

e) speech egocentrism (J.Piaje-egocentric speech).

Theories of speech generation

According to the analysis of theoretical and practical materials collected in the disciplines of psychology, psychophysiology, and psycholinguistics, the fusion of complex states in which acoustic speech signals are manifested as a result of complex coordinated actions is called a speech apparatus. Normally, the muscular movements of the lungs and respiratory body organs ensure an increase in pressure and the continuous participation of articulators in the speech act of air currents (internal and external).

2.2.1. Instrumental research methods

Multispiral computed tomography of the brain was performed in standard mode. The localization, nature, and dimensions of focal changes have been determined. The examination was carried out once on the day of admission.

2.2.2. Laboratory examination methods

All examined patients submitted the following set of laboratory tests at the time of admission and discharge: general and biochemical analysis of blood (C-reactive protein, sugar content, activated partial thrombin time (AQTV), prothrombin index, international normalized relations (MnO), coagulogram). Thus, the laboratory methods used in the study made it possible to reliably assess the biochemical composition of hemostasis, lipid metabolism, and blood. 2. 3. Methods of conducting rehabilitation measures In the rehabilitation department with the patient, a multidisciplinary brigade was formed, which included a neurologist, therapist, cardiologist, physiotherapist, attending physical education doctor, speech therapist, and neuropsychologist. The rehabilitation program is developed separately, taking into account the structure of neurological insufficiency and concomitant somatic pathology. To correct speech disorders, individual training with logopeds was carried out in the presence of cognitive disorders through group and individual training with a neuropsychologist. The choice of a set of exercises for the course of physical therapy was carried out jointly by a doctor, neurologist, and cardiologist in terms of their duration and intensity.

2.3. Statistical material processing

The results of the study were processed on a personal computer using methods of variational statistics. For statistical data processing, the Microsoft Office Excel-2013 software package was used, using the statistical processing functions installed using the STATISTICA-6.0 program. The statistical significance of the measurements obtained when comparing the average arithmetic (M), mean square deviation (SD), mean standard error (m), relative values (frequency,%), and mean values was determined by calculating the probability of error (P) when checking the normal distribution (on the ecstasy criterion) with the criterion of the Styudent (t) and by equality general dispersions (F-Fischer test). When comparing groups in terms of quality characteristics, we used the "2" criterion. To study the relationship between quantitative variables, correlation analysis with the calculation of Pearson's linear correlation coefficient was used. The p 0.05 reliability level was regarded as statistically significant.

CHAPTER III.

Clinical and pathogenetic properties of relapses

3.1. Comparative clinical and pathogenetic features of strokes

Our study found 1 patient (1.4%) in men between the ages of 18 and 44, 30 (52.5%) in the age range of 45–59, 28 (41.7%) in the age range of 60–74, and 3 (4.4%) in the age range of 75–90. At a significant level, patients between the ages of 45 and 59 were found to have a relatively high incidence of relapsed ischemic stroke. In the case of women, no relapsed ischemic stroke was observed between the ages of 18 and 44. There were 23 patients (56.3%) aged 45–59, 17 patients (41.3%) aged 60–74, and 1 patient (2.4%) aged 75–90, with significantly more recurrent ischemic stroke in women aged 45–59.

3.1 table

Comparative clinical features of recurrent strokes

	Patients with recurrent ischemic stroke		Patients with recurrent hemorrhagic stroke	
	Men (n=67) 62,03%	Women (n=41) 37,96%	Men (n=19) 65,51%	Women (n=10) 34,48%
18-44 years	1(1,4%)	0 (0%)	1 (0,5%)	0 (0 %)
45-59 years	35	23	9	2

	(52,5%)	(56,3%)	(47,3%)	(20%)
60-74 years	28 (41,7%)	17 (41,3%)	5 (26,3%)	5 (50%)
75-90 years	3 (4,4%)	1 (2,4%)	4 (21,1%)	3 (30%)

Male patients with relapsed hemorrhagic stroke accounted for 1 person (0.5%) between the ages of 18 and 44; bulgan bemos aged 45–59 were 9 (47.3%); 60–74 were 5 (56.3%); and 4 patients (21.1%) between the ages of 75–90. At a significant level, the frequency of re-hemorrhagic stroke in men aged 45–59 years was higher. Female patients with recurrent hemorrhagic stroke were not diagnosed with recurrent hemorrhagic stroke between the ages of 18 and 44. 2 patients (20%) between the ages of 45–59, 5 patients (50%) between the ages of 60–74, and 3 patients (30%) between the ages of 75–90 At the Achaemenid level, it is indicated that at the age of 60–74 years, this indicator is high.

Based on the results of our study, it can be seen that both types of stroke are dominated by patients of the male sex. Males are more susceptible to relapsed strokes than females. This distinction is weakened when considering age in women because, after the onset of menopause, women become a denominator in the protective effects of estrogens. For women over 45 years of age, this indicator decreases. In this case, the difference is justified by the properties of the IOC on the hormonal background itself. At this time, it was recognized that in men, on the other hand, relapsed strokes occur more often in older men at the expense of vascular insufficiency, a lack of physical movement, and the presence of risk factors.

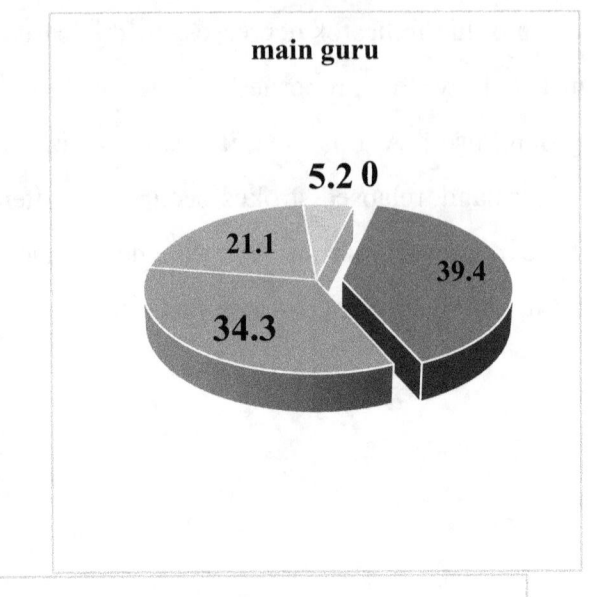

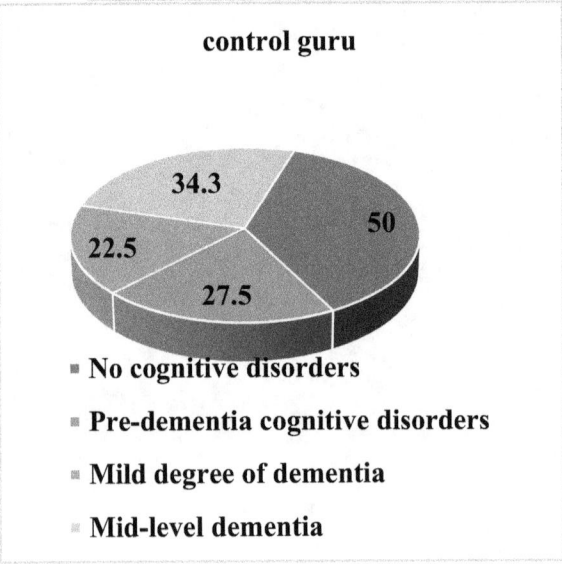

Figure 3.2. According to the results of the PSASS assessment, the level of cognitive deficit ($p<0.05$) in patients of different ages with stroke

3.2.- based on the data of the figure, it can be noted that the specificity of observations without cognitive distortions in the control group is higher than in the main group. Only mid-level dementia was observed in the main group. However, cognitive deficits have been found in 51.1% of the core group of patients and 58.8% of the control group.

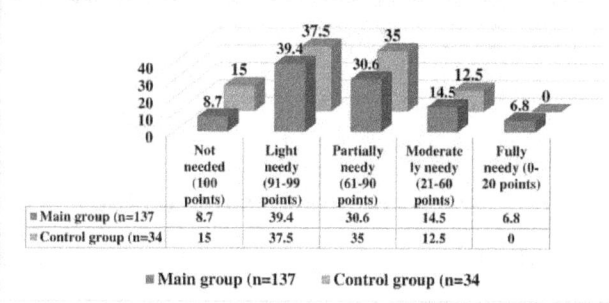

Figure 3.3 based on Bartel's assessment, the level of need for others in the daily lives of stroke patients (in scores, p>0.05)

On the Bartel Index, daily activities were evaluated when patients were admitted. (Figure 3.3). Both groups are dominated by light- to medium-sized observations that are not needed by others. The number of fully independent patients was higher in the control group. The Bukhara branch was transferred to the Department of Neurology at RSHTTYOIM to conduct a course of rehabilitation for 137 patients (100%) in the main group. The transfer of patients began the day they stabilized their condition. Rehabilitation events started from 9–14 days and included a course duration of 30–40 days.

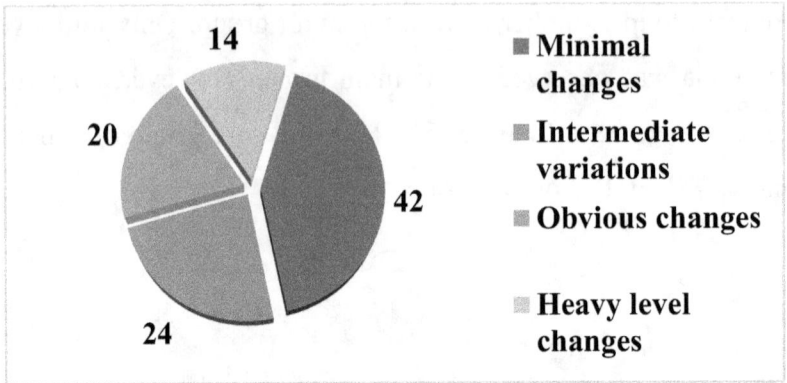

Figure 3.4. Severity of neurological deficits (in Ballard)in patients transferred to the rehabilitation unit according to the results of the NIHSS assessment

When transferred to the rehabilitation unit, the average score on the NIHSS scale is 8.59±8.15, PSASS - 25.88±3.23, Bartel - 78.62±25.11. Based on the results of the NIHSS scale neurological deficits assessment, patients were grouped for clarity. It appears that the majority of patients had minimal neurological changes.

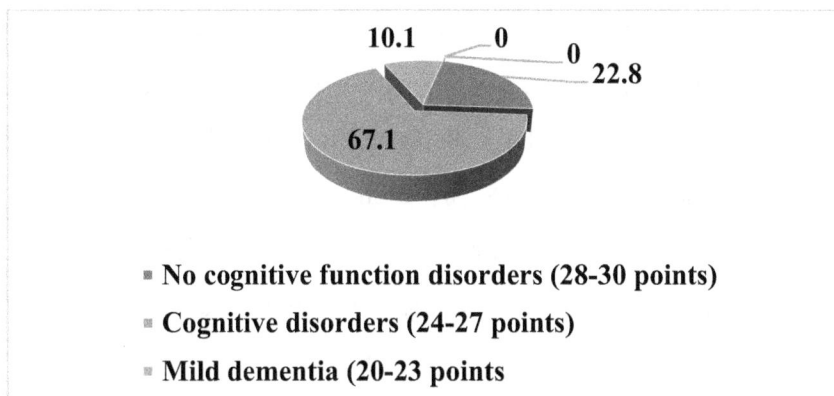

- No cognitive function disorders (28-30 points)
- Cognitive disorders (24-27 points)
- Mild dementia (20-23 points

Figure 3.5. Severity of cognitive impairment in patients (in points)up to the rehabilitation unit according to PSASS assessment results

Patients up to the rehabilitation unit in Figure 3.5 can be seen to be dominated by previous cognitive deficits.

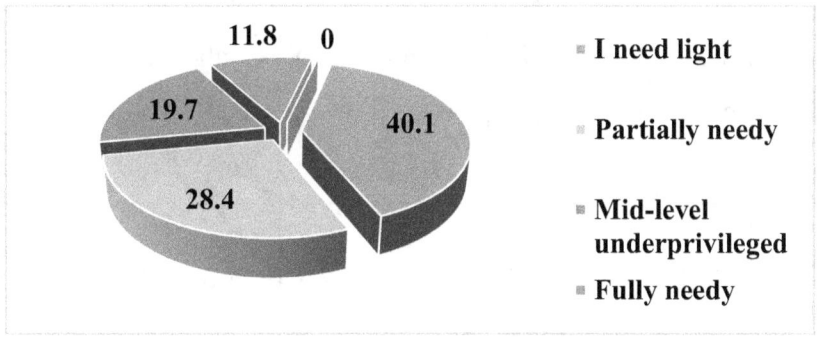

Figure 3.6. The level of need for others in the daily life of patients transferred to the rehabilitation unit according to the results of the assessment with the Bartel index(in points)

Thus, in the group of patients transferred to the rehabilitation unit, many had a degree of need for others. After being transferred to the rehabilitation unit, patients continued to receive the recommended hypotensive, cardial, antiagregant, and anticoagulant treatment measures in the neurology department, as well as completing the course of taking neuroprotective drugs.

Table 3.2

The most common neurological symptoms in the main and control groups are

NS	Age groups							
	18-44 years		45-59 years		60-74 years		75-90 years	
	Main group	Control group	Main group	Control group	Main group	Control group	Main group	Control group
A	8 (25,0%)	0 (0%)	8 (25,0%)	0 (0%)	12 (29,3%)	3 (25,0%)	8 (17,0%)	1 (6,7%)
AAS	3 (9,4%)	0 (0%)	3 (9,4%)	0 (0%)	11 (26,8%)	0 (0%)	9 (19,1%)	0 (0%)
MS	4 (12,5	1 (14,3	4 (12,5	1 (14,3	3 (7,3	0 (0%)	4 (8,5	0 (0%)

	%)	%)	%)	%)	%)		%)	
HG	7 (21,9 %)	2 (28,6 %)	7 (21,9 %)	2 (28,6 %)	13 (31,7 %)	9 (75,0 %)	24 (51,1 %)	1 (6,7 %)
H	15 (46,9 %)	2 (28,6 %)	15 (46,9 %)	2 (28,6 %)	24 (58,5 %)	8 (66,7 %)	31 (66,0 %)	5 (33,3 %)
M MP	23 (71,9 %)	3 (42,9 %)	23 (71,9 %)	3 (42,9 %)	26 (63,4 %)	10 (83,3 %)	34 (72,3 %)	10 (66,7 %)
GD	5 (15,6 %)	0 (0%)	5 (15,6 %)	0 (0%)	3 (7,3 %)	0 (0%)	7 (14,9 %)	0 (0%)
ARS	2 (6,3 %)	0 (0%)	2 (6,3 %)	0 (0%)	5 (12,2 %)	0 (0%)	8 (17,0 %)	0 (0%)
SLA	28 (87,5 %)	5 (71,4 %)	28 (87,5 %)	5 (71,4 %)	39 (95,1 %)	11 (91,7 %)	44 (93,6 %)	14 (93,3 %)

Note: NS - neurological syndrome, A – aphasia, AAS – apracto-agnostic syndrome, MS - meningeal symptoms, HG –

hemigipesthesia, H – hemiparesis, MMP - mimic muscle paresis, ARS - akinetic-rigid syndrome, SLA - statico-locomotor ataxia.

From schedule 3.2, it is known that the most common symptoms in the primary and control groups were statico-locomotor ataxia, with coordination disorders occurring significantly more frequently in patients with relapsed stroke in the 45–59 age group ($p < 0.05$), and in larger groups this difference was less pronounced. In the main group of patients, the manifestation of akinetic-rigid syndrome was observed, and its frequency increased with age, reaching 17% in the age group of 75–90 years. With a recurved disorder of cerebral circulation, these manifestations are more prominent due to a decrease in the compensatory reserves of the brain. Speech disorders were dominant in both groups at 75–90 years of age but were reliably frequent among patients with cerebral circulation impairment (p 0.05).

Table 3.3

Results of examination of patients on the PSASS scale of cognitive function during hospitalization

Checked day	Ischemia stroke		Hemorrhagic stroke	
	Primary (control group)	Backdated	Primary (control group)	Backdated

5-8	13,4±0,7	11,5±1,1	16,6±0,2	13,1±0,8
9-12	26,8±0,4	25,6±0,9	27,9±0,9	26,7±0,3
After 12 days	28,7±0,3	27,3±0,8	29,3±0,7	28,8±0,6

When divided by the results of the PSASS scale of patients in the main (n = 137) and control (n = 40) groups of different ages, only mid-level dementia was observed in the main group. There was an increase in the depth of cognitive deficits among patients in the main group with age; cognitive impairments were found (p 0.05).

3.2. Clinical picture of recurrent ischemic and hemorrhagic strokes depending on the pathogenetic subgroup

Clinical observations suggest that the pathogenetic subtype of primary strokes does not always correspond to the pathogenetic subtype of relapsed strokes. Among the 108 patients in the main group who suffered 137 relapsed strokes, the primary was ischemic stroke, and in 29 cases, hemorrhagic stroke.

Clinical forms of acute primary and recurrent disorders of cerebral circulation

The average development time for a relapsed ischemic stroke in the main group is 3.67±1.39 years, while hemorrhagic is 4.44±0.73 years, which is reliably abundant (p<0.05). The average age of patients with relapsed ischemic stroke was much higher compared to patients with relapsed hemorrhagic stroke (73.15 ± 4.10 and 70.37±3.89 years), it can be concluded that relapsed ischemic stroke after primary ischemic stroke is 94.4%, re-hemorrhagic stroke after hemorrhagic stroke (83.3%), i.e. ischemic stroke is more common than hemorrhagic stroke. Thus, risk factors for ischemia have great stability. It should be noted that in both cases, a lacunar infarction developed when it turned into a hemorrhagic and ischemic state, and in the transfusion of ischemic into a hemorrhagic state, hypertensive bleeding occurred in 5 cases, and in 1 case aneurysm rupture occurred. These examples probably combine the effects of such a risk factor as arterial hypertension. 6 cases were excluded, which turned ischemic stroke into hemorrhagic. In the presence of rare causes (vasculitis, antiphospholipid syndrome and venous thrombosis), the cause of relapsed strokes is consistent with the underlying cause. In addition, in some cases, hemodynamic and haemoreological strokes have recurred. The cardioembolic subtype of stroke recurred in 94.6% of patients, ranking first among recurrent disorders of circulation in the cranial brain. The prevalence of the cardioembolic subtype in patients who have had a re-stroke is associated with cardiac pathology, in which division fibrillation and arrhythmia are particularly important. The frequent repetition of the cardiovascular mechanism of vascular diseases determines the selection and intake of sufficient doses of anticoagulants in a promising direction of secondary prevention for this bloodthirsty of patients.

Atherothrombotic strokes are low-stable, relapsing in 86.4% of patients who have had a re-ischemic stroke. The largest polymorphism manifested in relation to a lacunar stroke: in only 76.5% of cases, recurrent disorders of cerebral circulation occurred in the same mechanism. The alternation of cardioembolic, atherothrombotic, and lacunar strokes shows the totality of a number of risk factors for these pathogenetic subtypes. The cause of relapsed hemorrhagic strokes usually indicates that it was the same as the primary stroke. Subarachnoidal hemorrhages were caused by an aneurysm without a branch, later re-rupturing the aneurysm. The tactics for treating patients with hemorrhagic stroke should be based on a close examination of the source of bleeding and an examination of the vascular canal to determine the causes of repeated damage. compared the viability of neurological deficits assessed on the NIHSS scale in the hospitalization of patients with the pathogenetic subtype of strokes.

Table 3.4

Results of assessment on the NIHSS scale on the pathogenetic subtype of recurrent ischemic strokes

NDAF	Ischemia stroke subtypes					HS
	CS	AS	L	H	GD	
MS	22 (40,7%)	10 (41,7%)	15 (88,2%)	3 (60,0%)	1 (100%)	11 (68,8%)
OC	21 (38,9%)	8 (33,3%)	2 (11,8%)	2 (40,1%)	0 (0%)	2 (12,5%)
IU	8 (14,8%)	5 (20,8%)	0 (0%)	0 (0%)	0 (0%)	1 (6,2%)
CC	3 (5,6%)	1 (4,2%)	0 (0%)	0 (0%)	0 (0%)	2 (12,5%)
Total	54 (100%)	24 (100%)	17 (100%)	5 (100%)	1 (100%)	16 (100%)

Note: NDAF-neurological deficits are found to be abnormal, MS- minimal changes (1-4 points), MCH - moderate changes (5-15 points), OC - obvious changes (16-20 points), CC - critical changes (21-42 points), HS – hemorrhagic stroke, CS – cardioembolic subtype, AS – atherothrombotic subtype, L –

lacunarctic type, H – hemorrhagic subtype, HS - hemodynamic subtype.

From Table 3.4, it can be seen that all pathogenetic subtypes of stroke in patients underwent minimal changes. Observations with cardioembolic, atherothrombotic, lacunar, and hemorrhagic strokes used statistical estimation methods. Compared to the severity of cardioembolic and atherothrombotic strokes, statistically significant differences were not found, despite the average NIHSS score being 0.05 and 9, respectively ($p > 0.05$). In addition to minimal changes in both groups, moderate and pronounced changes, as well as significant changes corresponding to the heavy flow of blood vessels, have been frequently identified. Cardioembolic strokes continue to cause the most pronounced neurological deficits. In the absolute majority of patients, lacunar strokes continue in mild form. Statistically significant differences have been found in comparison to cardioembolic and atherothrombotic sub-types (p 0.01). minimal neurological impairment and a positive prediction of the lacunar subtype is хос. The results of the tests showed that hemorrhagic strokes on the NIHSS scale averaged 2 points. Hemorrhagic strokes in the studied patient group were statistically much milder than cardioembolic strokes (p 0.05).

Table 3.5

The incidence of neurological symptoms in patients in the main group with different pathogenetic subtypes of stroke

NS	subtypes of ischemic stroke					GS (n=29)
	CS (n=60)	AS (n=31)	L (n=8)	GR (n=2)	GD (n=7)	
A	16 (29,6%)	4 (16,7%)	2 (11,8%)	3 (60,0%)	0 (0%)	2 (12,5%)
AAS	12 (22,2%)	6 (25,0%)	0 (0%)	2 (40,0%)	0 (0%)	2 (12,5%)
MS	5 (9,3%)	1 (4,2%)	0 (0%)	0 (0%)	0 (0%)	5 (31,3%)
GG	25 (46,3%)	10 (41,7%)	4 (23,5%)	1 (20,0%)	0 (0%)	5 (31,3%)
G	35 (64,8%)	17 (70,8%)	8 (47,1%)	2 (40,0%)	0 (0%)	7 (43,8%)
MMP	41 (75,9%)	17 (70,8%)	10 (58,8%)	4 (80,0%)	0 (0%)	10 (62,5%)
OM	9	3	1	0 (0%)	0 (0%)	2

B	(16,7%)	(12,5%)	(5,9%)			(12,5%)
APS	5 (9,3%)	4 (16,7%)	1 (5,9%)	2 (40,0%)	0 (0%)	0 (0%)
SLA	51(94,4%)	23(95,8%)	14(82,4%)	5 (100,0%)	1 (100,0%)	14(87,5%)

Note: NS-neurological syndrome, A-aphasia, AAS-apractoagnostic syndrome, MS-meningeal symptoms, HG-hemigipesthesia, G-hemiparesis, MMP – mimic muscle paresis, omb-oculomotor disorders, APS-akinetico-rigid syndrome, sla- statico-locomotor ataxia, ke – cardioembolic subtype, AT – atherotrombotic subtype, L – lacunar subtype, G hemorrhoeological subtype, GD – hemodynamic subtype, GI - hemorrhagic stroke.

From Table 3.5, it can be seen that the most frequent neurological sign for all pathogenetic subtypes is static-locomotor ataxia. It is important to note that patients with lacunar strokes have the lowest rates of ataxia. Ataxia is considered the only sign of hemodynamic strokes. Akinetico-rigid syndrome occurs in patients with subtypes of cardioembolic, atherothrombotic, lacunar, and hemorrhagic stroke. Extrapyramidal symptomatology has often been documented in the atherotrombotic subspecies of stroke.

Oculomotor disorders have been frequently identified in cardioembolic and atherotrombotic subtypes of ischemic stroke, as well as in hemorrhagic stroke patients. Mimic muscle paresis is the second-most common change after static-locomotor ataxia. On this basis, statistically reliable differences between groups were not identified. Hemiparesis and hemigipesthesia have often been reported in cardioembolic and atherothrombotic strokes, slightly less frequently in lacunar, hemorrheological, and hemodynamic strokes. Meningeal symptoms were found only in 31.3% of cases of hemorrhagic strokes, typical of the clinical picture.

It should be noted that in 9.3% of cases, clinical manifestations of meningial symptoms were detected in sudden and sharply developing cases. This debut of the disease occurred in cardioembolism and is usually associated with severe strokes: meningeal symptoms occurred in 1 out of 5 patients in a very severe condition, in 3 in severe condition, and in 1 in moderate weight. Atherothrombotic stroke has occurred in patients with apracto-agnostic syndrome and aphasia, as well as, a little less often, cardioembolic stroke. In general, the greatest variety of clinical symptoms was found in the cardioembolic and atherothrombotic sub-subtypes, which were characterized by being very severe. Subsequently, impaired locomotor functions have been analyzed as having the greatest influence on social readaptation and quality of life, which in turn reflects in detail the characteristics of movement and coordination disorders corresponding to the subtype of pathogenetic stroke. Muscle strength was assessed in the legs, contralateral to the lesion. Assessment on the Bartel scale showed that early data from the acute period differed significantly not only in the categorization of patients by gender but also when comparing groups as a whole. In dynamics on the Bartel scale, the increase in scores in the primary stroke group was much greater than in the re-stroke group (p 0.05) (table 3.7).

Table 3.6

Frequency of assessment of primary and re-stroke patients on the Bartel scale

Checked day	Ischemia stroke		Hemorrhagic stroke	
	Primary	Backdated	Primary	Backdated
5-8	22,4±2,2	18,7±1,8	20,2±1,8	12,3±1,7
9-12	38,7±1,8	25,7±2,1	40,3±2,1	28,2±1,9
After 12 days	52,3±1,2	28,3±1,9	60,3±1,1	33,5±1,8

Hemiparesis has not been found in patients with hemodynamic strokes. In patients with lacunar, hemorrhological, and hemorrhagic strokes, an advantage in sufficient muscle strength has been noted. The group of cardioembolic and atherothrombotic strokes was dominated by mild hemiparesis. In addition, the comparative weight of observations with intermediate hemiparesis in these two subspecies was very large. Deep hemiparesis was found in patients with cardioembolic, atherothrombotic, and hemorrhagic strokes (table 3.7).

Table 3.7

The incidence of neurological symptoms in patients in the main group with different pathogenetic subtypes of stroke

MSC		Ischemic stroke podtypes					HS (n=29)
		CS (n=60)	AS (n=31)	L (n=8)	H (n=2)	HDS (n=7)	
MS	GP	18(33,3%)	6 (25%)	9(52,9%)	3 (60%)	1(100%)	8 (50%)
	LH	19(35,2%)	11(45,8%)	7(41,2%)	2(40,0%)	0 (0%)	5 (31,3%)
	MH	8 (14,8%)	4 (16,7%)	1 (5,9%)	0 (0%)	0 (0%)	1 (6,2%)
	HP	9 (16,7%)	2 (8,3%)	0 (0%)	0 (0%)	0 (0%)	2 (12,5%)

M T	NT	22(40,7%)	8 (33,3%)	137(6,5%)	1 (20%)	1 (100%)	10 (62,5%)
	CT	2 (3,7%)	1 (4,2%)	0 (0%)	0 (0%)	0 (0%)	1 (6,2%)
	ATP-	25(46,3%)	11(45,8%)	3 (17,6%)	2(40,0%)	0 (0%)	5 (31,3%)
	ATE	1 (1,8%)	0 (0%)	0 (0%)	1(20,0%)	0 (0%)	0 (0%)
	AIM	4 (7,4%)	4 (16,7%)	1 (5,9%)	1 (20%)	0 (0%)	0 (0%)
SLA	LT	3 (5,6%)	1 (4,2%)	3 (17,6%)	0 (0%)	0 (0%)	2 (12,5%)
	S	8 (14,8%)	3 (12,5%)	3 (17,6%)	0 (0%)	0 (0%)	2 (12,5%)
	M	29 (53,7%)	13 (54,2%)	8 (47,2%)	3 (60%)	1 (100%)	9 56,3%)
	VE	14 (25,9%)	7 (29,1%)	3 (17,6%)	2 (40%)	0 (0%)	3 (18,7

							%)

Note: MSC – motion system characteristic, MS - muscle strength, MT – muscle tone, SLA - statico-locomotor ataxia, GP– hemiparesis absent 5 points, - light hemiparesis 4-5 points, MH – moderate hemiparesis 2-4 points, HP - hemiplegia. 0-2 points, NT - normotonia, ATP-ascending towards pyramidal type, ATE-ascending towards extrapyramidal type, AIM– ascending in mixed type, LT – low tone, S – slight, M –moderate, VE – vividly expressed, CS – cardioembolic subtype, AS – atherothrombotic subtype, L – lacunar subtype, H - hemorrheological subtype, HDS – hemodynamic subtype, HS-hemorrhagic stroke.

It is important to note that the cardioembolic subtype of stroke has revealed a high incidence of deep hemiparesis. The mean value of contralateral muscle strength in the legs from the center of injury was 4.0 for cardioembolic and atherothrombotic subtypes, 4.5 for hemorrhagic strokes, and 5.0 for lacunar, hemorrhoological, and hemodynamic strokes. At the same time, significant differences have been found in cardioembolic and lacunar strokes ($p < 0.05$), atherotrombotic and lacunar strokes (p 0.05), cardioembolic and hemorrheological strokes ($p < 0.05$), atherotrombotic, and hemorrheological strokes ($p < 0.05$). Examination and analysis of muscle tone have shown that in patients with cardioembolic, atherotrombotic, and hemorrhagic strokes, pyramidal hypertension is in most cases accompanied by hemiparesis. The highest number of paresis in lacunar strokes was not accompanied by tonality disturbances, and this difference is statistically reliable ($p < 0.05$). In many cases, statico-locomotor ataxia is expressed moderately between pathogenetic subtypes without statistically significant differences. Regardless of the pathogenesis of cerebral circulatory disorders, coarse coordination disorder occurs in vertebrobazillary furnace localization.

3.3. Features of the clinical course of relapsed ischemic and hemorrhagic strokes in patients who have undergone a stroke, depending on the focus of damage, gender, and age

Localization of the lesion furnace determines the severity of neurological insufficiency and compression reserve. In this context, the interposition of focal changes in primary and recurrent strokes is interesting. Below are the proportions of the clinical form and the localization of primary and recurrent disorders of cerebral circulation. According to the following, 83.3% of hemorrhagic strokes show homolateral recurrence in the right hemisphere, 16.7% of patients show hemorrhagic strokes in the left hemisphere, and lateralization occurs with hypertensive bleeding in another hemisphere. In all patients with hemorrhagic strokes in the left hemisphere, recurrent cranial disaster also developed on the left side, but in 50% of cases after hemorrhagic stroke, cases of ischemic stroke were present. Hemorrhagic strokes recur in 75% of cases.

Table 3.8

Distribution of primary and recurrent lesion foci with ischemic stroke by pathogenetic subtype of localization

UL	Инсульт типлари				
	CS	AS	LS	H	HS
RH –RH	9 (17,0%)	7 (26,3%	2 (25%)	0 (0%	2(28,5%)
RH – LH	3 (3,8%)	2(5,3%)	1 (12,2%)	0 (0%)	1 (14,2%)
RH – BVV	3 (5,7%)	0 (0%)	0 (0%)	0 (0%)	1 (14,2%)
LH– LH	23 (37,7%)	6 (21,0%)	2(25,0%)	0 (0%)	1 (14,2%)
LH – RH	2 (1,9%)	6 (26,3%)	1 (12,2%)	0 (0%)	1 (14,2%)
LH – VBP	4 (7,5%)	3(5,3%)	0 (0%)	0 (0%)	0 (0%)
VBP – VBP	8 (13,2%)	3 (5,3%)	1 (12,2%)	1 (50%)	1(14,2%)
VBP – RH	2 (3,8%)	4 (10,5%)	1 (12,2%)	0 (0%)	0 (0%)

VBP – LH	6 (9,4%)	0 (0%)	0 (0%)	1 (50%)	0 (0%)
Total	60 (100%)	31 (100%)	8 (100%)	2 (100%)	7 (100%)

Note: ul-primary and recurrent ischemia lesion localization, RH –Right hemisphere, LH – Left hemisphere, VBP –vertebrobazillary pool, CS – cardioembolic subtype, AS – atherotrombotic subtype, LS – lacunar subtype, H – hemorrheological subtype, HS - hemodynamic subtype.

Cardioembolic strokes were found in their own basin in 67.9% of cases; contralateral strokes in 32.1% of cases; atherotrombotic strokes were found in 52.6% of cases originating in the same vascular basin; right, left, and vertebrobasal strokes were observed; and strokes in 47.4% of cases were found to be bloodtrolateral strokes. In general, the differences between cardioembolic and atherothrombotic subtypes in the localization of primary and recurrent ischemic centers are considered statistically significant ($p < 0.05$).

On the NIHSS scale, a comparison of neurological deficits with primary and relapsed stroke localization was made. Patients with both primary and relapsed ischemic strokes in the cranial hemisphere experienced the most pronounced neurological impairment.

Table 3.9

Assessment on the NIHSS scale, taking into account the localization of damage to primary and recurrent strokes

HD	Localization of primary and recurrent stroke								
	RH – RH	RH LH	RH-VB P	LR-LR	LR -RH	LH-VB P	VB P-VB P	VB P - RH	VB P-LH
Min Ch	8 37,1%	4 62,5%	2 66,7%	14 42,5%	6 60,0%	4 55,6%	11 84,1%	5 75,0%	4 60,0%
MC	6 29,6%	3 37,5%	1 33,3%	14 42,5%	2 20,0%	3 33,3%	2 10,5%	0 0%	2 20,0%
OCh	5 25,9%	0 0%	0 0%	2 6,8%	1 10%	1 11,1%	1 5,4%	3 25,0%	2 20,0%
CC	1 7,4%	0 0%	0 0%	2 6,8%	1 10%	0 0%	0 0%	0 0%	0 0%
Total	20 100%	7 100%	3 100%	32 100%	10 100%	7 100%	14 100%	7 100%	7 100%

Note: HD - neurological deficits occur at 14 output levels, MinCH–minimum changes (1-4 points), MC - mean changes (5-15 points), OCh– obvious changes (16-20 points), CC - critical changes (21-42 points), RH-right hemisphere, LH – left hemisphere, VBP-vertebrobazillary pool

In patients with a stroke in the right hemisphere, the average value of the NIHSS scale in terms of the number of points is the largest. These changes are consistent with ideas that there are differences in the pathogenesis of stroke in different hemispheres. With the change in lateralization, statistically reliably relapsed strokes led to fewer neurological deficits: in the right hemisphere ($p < 0.01$), in the left ($p < 0.05$). Among patients with ipsilateral primary and recurrent stroke, there is a deep neurological deficiency, which is explained by the formation of a new ischemia zone around glial-atrophic changes. Nevertheless, these groups also have patients with mild neurological deficits. Apparently, they had a complete regression of symptoms after a primary stroke brain disaster, but the recovery after a relapsed stroke due to decreased neuroplasticity was minimized. Patients with primary stroke in the contralateral hemisphere often die during the acute period of relapsed stroke.

Table 3.10

The degree of occurrence of neurological symptoms in patients of the main group, taking into account the localization of damage

NS	Localization of primary and recurrent stroke								
	RH RH (n=20)	RH LH (n=7)	RH VB P (n=3)	LH LH (n=32)	LH RH (n=10)	LH VB P (n=7)	VBP VBP (n=14)	VB P RH (n=7)	VB P LH (n=7)
A	0 0%	1 12,5%	0 0%	20 54,1%	1 12,5%	5 55,5%	0 0%	0 0%	1 20,0%
AAS	9 33,3%	3 37,5%	0 0%	7 18,9%	2 25,0%	3 33,3%	0 0%	0 0%	0 0%
MS	2 7,4%	1 12,5%	1 33,3%	3 8,1%	2 25,0%	0 0%	0 0%	0 0%	2 40,0%
HG	12 44,4%	2 25,0%	2 66,7%	14 37,8%	2 25,0%	3 33,3%	6 31,6%	1 25,0%	1 20,0%
HP	20 74,1	5 62,5	2 66,7	24 64,9	4 50,0	3 33,3	6 31,6	1 25,0	2 40,0

	%	%	%	%	%	%	%	%	%
MMP	19 70,4%	6 75,0%	3 100%	28 75,7%	3 37,5%	6 66,7%	9 47,4%	3 75,0%	3 60,0%
OMD	3 11,1%	2 25,0%	0 0%	8 21,6%	0 0%	0 0%	2 10,5%	0 0%	1 20,0%
ARS	2 7,4%	3 37,5%	1 33,3%	1 2,7%	1 12,5%	0 0%	4 21,1%	0 0%	0 0%
SLA	25 92,6%	8 100%	3 100%	33 89,2%	7 87,5%	8 100%	15 78,9%	4 100%	4 80,0%

Note: NS-neurological syndrome, A-aphasia, AAS-apractoagnostic syndrome, MS-meningeal symptoms, HG-hemigipesthesia, HP - hemiparesis, MMP-mimic muscle paresis, OMD – oculoomotor disorders, ARS - akinetic-rigid syndrome, SLA - statico-locomotor ataxia. LH-in the left hemisphere, RH-in the right hemisphere.

Static-locomotor ataxia occurred in most patients without statistically significant differences depending on the location of the center. Akinetico-rigid syndrome was consistent with ideas about the possibility of Parkinson's syndrome in these relapsed foci. Interestingly, akinetico-rigid syndrome occurs when the skull is in at least two pools of blood circulation. Hemiparesis has been reported in most cases of hemispheric strokes and has often occurred with ipsilateral localization of the recurved center. Apracto-agnostic syndrome appeared without statistically significant differences in both right and left hemisphere strokes and lateralization variation. Aphasia was noted in cases of damage to the left hemisphere with brain damage in a primary or relapsed stroke. Statistically significantly more frequent speech disorders ($p < 0.05$) compared to other groups were observed when the primary and control Guru were positioned on the left in a stroke. The mutual location of primary and recurrent strokes largely determines the state of the cognitive sphere. To evaluate it, an assessment and comparison were carried out on the PSASS scale, taking into account the localization of vascular damage. The results are reflected in Table 3.11.

Table 3.11

Results of evaluation on the xolda PSASS scale, taking into account the localization of primary and recurrent strokes

CD	Localization of primary and recurrent stroke								
	RH	RH-LH	RH VB P	LH LH	LH RH	LH VB P	VB P VB	VB P RH	VB P LH
RH-RH									

						P			
NCI	6 30%	4 57,5%	2 66,7%	13 40,6	3 30,0	2 33,3%	7 52,6%	5 75,0%	5 60,0%
PCI	5 25%	2 28,0%	1 33,3%	8 25%	5 50%	4 55,6%	6 42,1%	2 25,0%	1 20,0%
MidGD	9 45%	1 14,5%	0 0%	9 28,1%	2 20%	1 11,1%	1 5,3%	0 0%	1 20,0%
MGD	1 3,7%	0 0%	0 0%	2 6,3%	0 0%	0 0%	0 0%	0 0%	0 0%
SGD	0 0%	0 0%	0 0%	0 0%	0 0%	0 0%	0 0%	0 0%	0 0%
Total	21 100%	7 100%	3 100%	32 100%	10 100%	7 100%	14 100%	7 100%	7 100%

Note: CD-cognitive deficit, NCI-no cognitive impairment (score 28-30), PCI-pre-dementia cognitive impairment (score 24-27), MidGD –mild Grade dementia (score 20-23), MGD – moderate grade dementia (score 11-19), SGD –severe grade dementia (Score 0-10), RH-right hemisphere, LH-left hemisphere.

It is known from our study that in patients with strokes in the main and control group of the hemisphere, the most pronounced cognitive disorders were recorded. These groups were dominated by patients with predicament disorders and mild degrees of dementia, only they also had patients with moderate dementia. A slightly deeper cognitive deficit has been found with the right hemisphere localization of the furnace.

Statistically significant differences were found in these groups compared to cranial hemisphere damage ($p<0.01$ in the right hemisphere, $p<0.01$ in the left hemisphere).

The severity of the manifestation of recurrent ipsilateral strokes is mainly due to a decrease in the availability of reserves in the hemisphere. Compensating for impaired cognitive function is only possible due to interhemispheric connections, which means that in patients aged 45–59 years, interhemispheric relationships have a number of characteristics, with neuroplasticity potential generally reduced.

3.4. Practical study of speech and thinking

Clinical and neuropsychological examinations have shown that in 1–5 days of treatment, cerebral edema events occurred after the relief of cerebral insufficiency, that is, at the end of the acute period. The study was usually conducted every 20–30 minutes.

The simplest, but sufficient, methods were used, subject to the rules of research. Sixteen small subtest results from a standardized speech analysis using neuropsychological methodology (CHM) were studied. The characteristics of these disorders and of patients with various lateralizations (right and left hemispheres) in the post-stabilization period of the expressed clinical condition were compared with the regression of the clinical signs defining speech. In our study, 67 out of 108 patients had spontaneous and dialytic speech disorders in 62.03%, compared to 41 female patients; 22 in 20.37%, compared to 45 out of 67; and 41.66% of re-ischemic patients had spontaneous and dialytic, i.e., the patient had difficulty answering questions, was unable to answer questions asked, and was more common in men than women.

Automated speech was reported in 37.03% of 40 out of 108 patients, of which 12 (11.11%) were observed in women with ischemic stroke, and 28 times (25.92%) in men with ischemic stroke were found to be twice as high in men as women. In automated speech, patients perform nods, negations, and gestures instead of answering "yes" or "no" to sentences or questions asked. Repetition of common words occurred in 11.11% of 12 out of 108 patients, of which 1 in 0.92% was found in women and 11 out of 67 in men (10.18%). Repetition of words in 20 out of 108 patients with re-ischemic stroke

(18.51%) caused 3 out of 3 women with re-ischemic stroke, 2.77%, and 15.74% of 17 out of 67 men with re-ischemic stroke to even have difficulty uttering what was said. This, too, is more common in men compared to women. Artistic speech was 52.77% out of 57 out of 108 patients, compared to 28 for women diagnosed with ischemic stroke at 25.92%, while artistic speech pronunciation was impaired at 26.85% for 29 out of 67 men with re-ischemic stroke, which was also found to be twice as much in men as in women. The rate of speech was 55.55% in 60 of 108 patients, compared to 12 (11.11%) in women with ischemic stroke and 48 (44.44%) in men, which was also more common in men compared to women. In listening, 15 out of 108 patients reported 13.88%, of which 1 in women had 0.92% of patients with re-ischemic stroke, 14 in men had 12.96%, and more in men compared to women. In terms of speech softness, 60 out of 108 patients were observed, or 55.55%, of which 9 were 8.33% in women with ischemic stroke and 47.22% in men compared to 51 in women. Tone speech occurred in 73.14% of 79 patients out of 108, in 31 (28.7%) women and 48 (44.44%) men. Melodious speech disorders have been observed. Comprehensible natural speech occurred in 12.96% of 14 out of 108 patients, of which females with ischemic stroke had intelligible natural speech disorder in 2.77% of 3 and 10.18% of 11 in men. Speech line retention was 53.7% in 58 out of 108 patients, of whom 19 were 17.59% women and 36.11% men with impaired speech line retention. The automatic counting process was observed in 55.55% of 60 out of 108 patients, of which 13 were 12.03% women and 47 were men, with 43.51% having impaired automatic counting. Oral Praxis Disorder was observed in 60 out of 108 patients (55.55%), 6.48% in 7 women, and 49.07% in 53 men. Of the 108 patients familiar with the cheeks of close people, 48 had 44.44%, of which 11 had 10.18% in women and 34.26% in men, and there were cases of not recognizing their relatives, even their own children, and not remembering their names. Alien detection was 56.48% in 61 out of 108 patients, of which 19 were 17.59% women and 38.88% were 42 men. Actual spatial orientation speech was 13.88% in 15 out of 108 patients, of which 5.55% in 6 patients were women and 9 in 8,335 were men.

Figure 3.9. Frequency of occurrence of speech disorders in women and men in primary hemorrhagic stroke (in%)

In our study, spontaneous and dialytic speech in patients with re-hemorrhagic stroke was observed in 14 out of 29 patients at 48.27%, of which 3 were women at 10.34% and 11 were men at 11.93%. Automated speech occurred in 44.82% of 13 patients out of 29, of whom 5 in 17.24% were women and 8 in 27.58% were men. Artistic speech occurred in 62.06% of 18 patients out of 29, of whom 20.68% were women and 41.38% were men.

Simple verbal repetition was observed in 29 patients (27.58% in 8 patients), of whom 3.44% were female and 24.13% were male. Word repetition was found in 27.58% of 8 patients out of 29, of which 6.89% were observed in 2 patients in women and 20.69% in 6 patients in men. Simple verbal repetition was observed in 29 patients (27.58% in 8 patients), of whom 3.44% were female and 24.13% were male. Speech softness was 65.51% in 19 patients out of 29, of whom 27.58% were women and 11 were men (37.93%). Listening memory test performance was 24.13% in 7 patients out of 29, of whom 3.44% were women and 20.68% were men. Speech softness was 65.51% in 19 patients out of 29, of whom 27.58% were women and 11.93% were men. Speech tempo was observed in 58.62% of 17 out of 29 patients, of which 9 in women were observed in 31.03% and 8 in men in 27.58%. Melodious speech disorders were observed in 13 patients out of 29, with 44.82% of cases, of which 17.24% were observed in 5 patients in women and 27.58% in 8 patients in men. Comprehensible natural speech disorder was observed in 14 patients out of 29 patients, with a prevalence of 48.27%, of which 10.34% was observed in 3 patients in women and 37.93% in 11 patients in men. Speech line maintenance disorders were observed in 19 patients out of 29, with 65.51% of cases, of which 24.13% were observed in 7 patients in women and 41.38% in 12 patients in men.

Violation of the automatic counting process was observed in 19 patients out of 29, with 65.51% of cases, of which 24.13% were observed in 7 Nafar patients in women and 41.38% in 12 patients in men. Disorders of oral praxis were observed in 18 patients out of 29, with 62.06% of cases, of which 5 patients in women had 17.24% and 13 patients in men had 44.82%. Near-human facial recognition disorders were observed in 23 patients out of 29, with 79.31% of cases, of which 27.58% were reported in 8 patients in women and 51.72% in 15 patients in men. Alien recognition disorders were observed in 23 patients out of 29 patients, 79.31% of whom were observed in 31.03% of 9 patients in women and 48.27% of 14 patients in men. Actual maqon disorientation was observed in 12 patients out of 29, with 41.38% of cases, of which 10.34% were observed in 3 patients in women and 31.03% in 9 patients in men. Information about the patient's speech is determined during a conversation or through special examinations. Speech can also be checked by repeating simple and complex words. Speech disorders are also diagnosed using neuropsychological tests. The following disorders of speech are noted in the conclusion: afferent motor aphasia, efferent motor aphasia, sensory aphasia, acoustic-mnestic aphasia, amnestic aphasia, semantic aphasia, dynamic aphasia, fainting, stuttering, dysarthria, and dyslalia. A comparison of observations from the baseline and control groups revealed some features of relapsed strokes in patients. With an increase in age, the proportion of patients with recurrent ishemiki strokes in the main group increased. There was a difference in the composition of the pathogenetic types of primary and recurrent strokes: between primary strokes, the atherotrombotic subtype recurs if the first cardioembolic subtype prevails (p 0.05). Attention should also be paid to the high specificity of lacunar strokes among brain disasters in relapsed stroke. In a comparative analysis of the localization of the primary and relapsed centers, no statistically significant differences were found ($p > 0.05$), with hemispheric strokes dominating all age groups. Some features of the clinical course of relapsed stroke have been identified. Observations with clear and critical neurological deficits on the NIHSS scale have been extensive in the main group above. In relapsed stroke, age affects the depth of neurological deficits ($p < 0.05$).

The risk factors for ischemic stroke have been found to be much more stable compared to hemorrhagic stroke. The alternation of cardioembolic, atherothrombotic, and lacunar strokes shows the totality of a number of risk factors for these pathogenetic subgroups. According to the clinical picture, relapsed atherothrombotic strokes were not inferior in weight to cardioembolic strokes. In the absolute majority of patients, lacunar strokes continued in mild form. It is worth noting that hemorrhagic strokes are very mild. Comparing the clinical course of strokes with different localizations of the center, patients experiencing primary and recurrent ischemic injury in one hemisphere experienced the most neurological impairment, and right-hemisphere strokes were more severe than those in the left hemisphere ($p < 0.05$). This category of patients is also characterized by pronounced cognitive disorders. Statistically, relapsed strokes with lateralization changes have resulted in fewer neurological deficits ($p < 0.05$).

The conclusion was that the risk factors for relapsed stroke in 137 patients and the features of their rehabilitation period were studied. 137 patients who had suffered a relapsed stroke over a period of 5 years formed the core group. The control group consists of 40 patients who suffered a single stroke five years ago. Patients were observed in the conditions of the resuscitation and neurology departments of the Bukhara branch of RSHTTYOIM. The condition of patients is described using scale methods. Neurological status was assessed on the NIHSS (National Institutes of Health Stroke Scale), daily activity (Bartel index), intellectual and mnestic disorders (PSASS scale), and the Rankin scale (functional disability level). In the neurology department, all patients received therapy according to medical and economic standards to manage the acute period of stroke. The localization, size, and nature of the primary and recurrent pathological fly were evaluated by conducting CT, MPT, and laboratory methods, which made it possible to reliably assess the state of hemostasis, lipid metabolism, and blood biochemical composition. Rehabilitation treatment provided by the Department of Neurology was received by the main group of patients. The duration of rehabilitation treatment is 40 days. At the time of admission, rehabilitation measures were carried out, taking into account the structure of the neurological insufficiency. Sessions with electrical stimulation, phototherapy, balneotherapy, exercise therapy, acupuncture, speech correction, and a neuropsychologist were used. The severity of neurological deficits was assessed on the day of reception and response using the NIHSS, Rankin, Rivermid, and Bartel scales. The results of the study were processed on a personal computer using variational statistics. In our study, the likelihood of developing RE-strokes increased with age; about 80% of cerebrovascular pathology developed in patients aged 45–59 years. The problem of acute cerebrovascular diseases in patients aged 45–59 is becoming relevant against the background of an increase in the average life expectancy of the population: by 2025, the number of people over 60 in the world will reach 1.2 billion. Without qualified preventive measures, recurrent cerebrovascular diseases increase by about nine times.

The high prevalence of relapsed stroke among people aged 45–59 necessitates the need for a complete study of risk factors for this condition. Many studies have been devoted to the study of risk factors for circulatory disorders in the acute brain, but re-strokes in Haki still do not have enough information in the literature. In addition to relapsed stroke, people aged 45–59 often have a combination of pathological conditions that not only join together but also strengthen each other, resulting in circulatory disorders. Identifying the most important risk factors for recurrent or refractory cranial circulatory disorders in patients aged 45–59 with somatic disorders is one of the goals of this study. The course of stroke in people aged 45–59 years and the biochemical reactions that occur in damaged brain tissue are also characterized by a number of features. As age progresses, it causes the accumulation of a number of functional disorders in the central nervous system, which leads to further decompensation of cerebral circulation. Age-related changes in the immune system determine the transition to anti-inflammatory reactions.

IV-CHAPTER.

Comparative significance of the results of laboratory and neurovisual examinations in patients with recurrent ischemic and hemorrhagic stroke

4.1. Comparative importance of risk factors for relapsed strokes in patients

The specific characteristics of patients with re-stroke are placenta somatic pathology and chronic comorbid diseases, which are dangerous factors that cause circulatory disorders in the cranial brain. These conditions also affect its course and prediction. The role of each of the risk factors in the regulation of blood circulation in the brain is individual. In addition, somatic comorbid conditions complicate the course of the disease by generalizing each other's complications. A long-term increase in arterial pressure leads to a number of metabolic syndromes and a change in the endothelial structure of the vascular wall, which in turn leads to a violation of the central and peripheral circulation. As a result of the years, arterial hypertension increases from 1 level to 2–3 degrees, and later, arterial hypertension, in combination with dyslipidemia, causes the origin of atherosclerosis.

All patients of the main and control groups were previously treated with a diagnosis of hypertension. The duration of the course of the disease is 15.4±6.1 years in the main group, and 13.8±5.8 years in the control group without statistically significant differences (p>0.05). No AH 1 levels were observed in both primary and control group patients, 14.1% - AH 2 levels, 63.2% - AH 3 levels, 4.4% of patients in the control group were found to be AH 2 levels, and 18.1% were found to be AH 3 levels. It should be said that in relapsed ischemic and hemorrhagic strokes, very high blood pressure was found, which in turn leads to damage to target organs and impaired autoregulation of blood circulation in the brain. At the same time, 22.5% of the control group, 77.8% of the main group, were taking antihypertensive drugs before they had a stroke and a re-stroke. Patients in the re-stroke group had relatively high blood pressure rates over the past 5 years ($p < 0.01$).

In the primary and control group, it was found that the increase in patients with levels AH 2 and AH 3 is more likely to be observed only in patients aged 45-59 years. The maximum difference in patients with re-stroke was observed among those over 45-59 years of age when considering their age groups. It is known that increased changes due to the thickening of the endothelium of the vascular wall, on the scale of the decrease in the autoregulation Depot, an increase in blood pressure, begin to play an important role as a risk factor for blood vessels (table 4.1)

4.1 - table

Distribution of major (n=108) ischemic, (n=29) hemorrhagic and Control (n=20) ischemic, (n=20)hemorrhagic groups by age and AH levels of patients

AH	Age groups							
	18-44 years		45-59 years		60-74 years		75-90 years	
	Main group	Control group	Main group	Control group	Main group	Control group	Main group	Control group
AH 2 degree	2 (1.1%)	2 (1.1%)	3 (1,7%)	2 (1.1%)	12 (6,8%)	2 (1.1%)	8 (4,5%)	2 (1.1%)
AH 3 degree	4 (2.3%)	6 (3,4%)	36 (20,3%)	6 (3,4%)	47 (26,5%)	14 (7,9%)	25 (14,1%)	6 (3,4%)
Total	6 (3,4%)	8(4,5%)	39(22,2%)	8(4,5%)	59(33,3%)	16(9,0%)	33(18,6%)	8 (4,5%)

A comparison was made with the pathogenetic subgroup, which allowed the most careful control of this indicator and the identification of groups of patients in need of correction (table 4.2).

4.2 - table

Strokes of patients in the main group (n=137) are pathogenetic small distribution by type and AH leve

AH degree	Pathogenetic type of ischemic stroke						HS
	CS	AS	LS	HSub	BS	general ischemic	
AH 2 degree	12(11,1%)	8(7,4%)	3(2,8%)	1(0,9%)	2(1,8%)	26(24%)	5(17,2)
AH 3 degree	48(44,4%)	23(21,3%)	5(4,6%)	1(0,9%)	5(4,6%)	82(76%)	24(82,8%)
Total	60(55,6%)	31(28,7%)	8(7,4%)	2(1,8%)	7(6,5%)	108(100%)	29(100%)

Note: HS-hemorrhagic stroke, CS–cardioembolic subtype, AS-atherothrombotic subtype, LS – lacunar subtype,

HSub-hemorrheological subtype, BS- blood-flow subtype, RF - rare factors, AH-arterial hypertension.

Most patients with cardioembolic strokes are seen to suffer from AH 2 levels. In this group, the cause of strokes is one or more cardiac pathologies, and in most cases, Olma fibrillation. Among patients with atherothrombotic stroke, most suffered from the level of AH 3, a group that was statistically significantly different from its predecessor ($p<0.05$). It is noteworthy that in patients with lacunar stroke, the comparative severity of patients with AH levels of 3 was the lowest. Finally, hemorrhagic strokes, especially hypertensive bleeding, are associated in most cases with AH 3 levels, which coincides with ideas about this type of pathogenesis of cerebral circulation disorders.

The next risk factor is olamacha fibrillation. The occurrence of strokes as a result of umbilical fibrillation develops 5 times more frequently than the average population (Bokeria L, 2005). In addition, episodes of cardioembolia tend to recur, resulting in severe neurological failure or death.

The rate of occurrence of cardiac fibrillation spread increases depending on the age of the patients. This trend is reflected in the main and control groups of patients. Among all patients with re-stroke in the main group, the displacement of relapsed embolus in biliary fibrillation is more common than in the control group (p<0.05). Constant-form paroxysmal fibrillation dominated both the main body and the control group. Specificity in the paroxysmal form has been higher in patients with relapsed stroke, but this trait is statistically irrelevant (p>0.05). According to the literature, in about 30% of patients with a paroxysmal form lasting 2-3 years, fibrillation occurs in a permanent form, and over time the risk of stroke becomes maximum (Bokeria La, 2005). Comparative heart rate analysis of primary and control group patients suffering from bladder fibrillation has been conducted.

All analysis showed that adequate administration of warfarin was observed to reduce the risk of cardioembolic stroke by 68% and aspirin intake by only 16%. In relation to this category of patients, the use of alternative antiagregant drugs with the drug Plavix has not been sufficiently studied. Patients with kidney fibrillation in the main group of patients were prescribed the drug warfarin for 4 patients, but it was found that patients did not take the drug. We looked at which of the patients took warfarin and which led to an MNO-dependent examination of the amount of the drug. It appears that 37.5% of bladder fibrillation with a permanent form, while 28.6% of patients with a paroxysmal form received warfarin. In a similar procedure, 12.5% and 4.8% of patients received alternative anticoagulants (csarelto, raxaben). Most patients took aspirin. In general, patients with a paroxysmal form of bladder fibrillation were characterized by a lower need for anticoagulants. The optimal MNO values for patients with an irregular form of biliary fibrillation are 2.0-3.0. In only 5 patients from the main group and 1 patient from the control group, the MNO matched the recommended level when hospitalized. The average MNO rate among patients taking warfarin was 1.70±1.32. Thus, the Prevention of thromboembolic complications was not effective enough in the main group. There are a number of explanations for this. Taking warfarin requires regular control of the MNO, while disabled patients, especially stroke patients, often cannot go to the Polyclinic to donate blood. This forces them to give up taking the medication to avoid hemorrhagic complications or to take them uncontrollably. Alternatively anticoagulants i.e. csarelto,raxaben is a very expensive drug. In addition, age-related cognitive changes prevent the drug from being prescribed, as well as reduce craving for treatment

Table 4.3

Reception of drugs in the permanent form of biliary fibrillation and paroxysmal forms of biliary fibrillation

The drug	Division fibrillation constant form		Division fibrillation paroxysmal form	
Warfarin	12	37,5%	6	28,6%
Xarelto	1	3,1%	0	0%

Pradaxa	3	9,4%	1	4,8%
Plavix	3	9,4%	4	19,0%
Aspirin	12	37,5%	9	42,8%
Not accepted	1	3,1%	1	4,8%
Total	32	100%	21	100%

It should be remembered that in addition to Olma fibrillation, there are a number of other factors that can cause cardioembolic stroke. The main group includes mitral valve stenosis, endocarditis, post-valve prosthesis condition, presence of a pacemaker, left ventricular aneurysm. The assessment of the level of risk of each of these factors was carried out by the method of multi-factor analysis.

Paroxysmal form of bladder fibrillation followed by the presence of mitral valve stenosis and pacemaker and persistent form of bladder fibrillation and increased risk of developing cardioembolic strokes. At the same time, maximum attention should be paid to the Fibrillation of the bladder due to the high prevalence among the elderly contingent.

4.2. Analysis of the results of laboratory and neurovisual examinations

Diabetes is an independent risk factor for relapsed strokes, which in many ways increases its severity. 25 (20.8%) patients in the main group and 7 (20.6%) patients in the control group were diagnosed with Type 2 diabetes. The remaining patients were found to have elevated sugar levels for the first time. The duration of the disease is 20.7±8.1 years in the main group and - 18.9±14.3 years in the control group, without statistically significant differences (p>0.05). Showed age gradation of the main and control groups of patients with diabetes.

Table 4.4

Distribution of observations of the main and control groups with diabetes by age

Age groups								
18-44 years		45-59 years		60-74 years		75-90 years		
Main group (n=6)	Control group (n=8)	Main group (n=39)	Control group (n=8)	Main group (n=59)	Control group (n=16)	Main group (n=33)	Control group (n=8)
0	0	8(20,5%)	2(5,1%)	16(41%)	5(12,8%)	6(15,4%)	5(12,8)

In the basic as well as control group, the level of detection of diabetes was carried out according to age. During the acute period of their strokes, blood glucose levels can increase not only in patients with diabetes, but also in other patients due to a non-хос stress reaction to the body itself. The levels of sugar received among patients of the main and control groups were analyzed. In the control group, Anamnesis had an average glucose level of 5.34±0.57 mmol/l in non-diabetic patients, with slightly higher average levels in confirmed diagnosed patients, 6.78±1.59 mmol/l, but this difference is not statistically significant (p>0.05). In the main group, these indicators were 5.94±1.29 and 8.15±2.38 mmol/l, respectively. Patients with diabetes have significantly higher glucose levels in relapsed strokes (p<0.01). In addition, hyperglycemia above 15 mmol/l was recorded in 3 patients, which is a prognostic negative sign. Therefore, patients with diabetes mellitus with recurrent stroke in the acute period have a much higher level of glycemia. To assess the lipid spectrum of patients with Type 2 diabetes, the coefficient of atherogenicity was analyzed. The difference between diabetic and non-diabetic patients is statistically reliable (p<0.05) in the relapsed stroke group by atherogenicity factor. In the presence of diabetes mellitus, the value of the atherogenicity coefficient is much higher (4.07±0.30 and 3.50±0.14). The differences in the atherogenicity coefficient in the control group are statistically unreliable (3.01±0.68 and 2.87 ± 0.21). Thus, although the comparative severity of diabetes patients in the primary and control groups is similar, in the primary group the disease continued with deeper metabolic disorders. A comparison was made on the NIHSS scale to assess the clinical status of blood vessels in patients with diabetes mellitus. The average score among patients in the control group with diabetes was 10.71±6.6, while the average score for patients without diabetes was 5.84±5.48. However, these differences are not statistically significant (p>0.05). In the core group, the NIHSS averages were 12.36±11.58 and 6.13±5.44, respectively, with strokes in diabetic patients becoming statistically significantly more severe (p<0.01). 4 out of 6 patients with critical neurological deficits; 9 (21-42 points) reported impaired carbohydrate metabolism.

Excess body weight is also a risk factor for acute circulatory disorders of the brain, increasing the load on the cardiovascular system, and indicates a number of metabolic dysfunctions, reflecting the proportions of patients with different body mass indices (TMI) in the main and control groups.

Table 4.5

Distribution of patients in the primary (n=137) and Control (n=40) group by body mass index

Taya mass index	Main group (n=137)		Control group (n=40)	
	Abs. n	%	Abs. n	%
<25 (norm	47	35,8	20	50,0
25-30 (took obesity)	27	19,2	9	23,5
30-35 (obesity 1 degree)	38	29,2	6	17,6
35-40 (semizlik2daraja)	19	13,3	5	8,8
>40 (obesity 3 degrees)	6	2,5	-	0
Total	1 37	100	40	100

According to this criterion, the difference between the primary and control groups was statistically reliable ($p<0.05$). In the control group, half of the patients had normal body weight and no obesity 3 levels were reported. In the main group, about a third of patients did not have excess body weight, and 6 patients reported 3 levels of obesity. One of the reasons for this difference is lifestyle changes after a stroke, hypodynamics, often only the possibility of movement within the room boundary. Clinical and biochemical signs of the risk of developing ischemic and hemorrhagic strokes. The period of acute vascular damage depends on the size of the brain tissue, the premorbid state, comorbid somatic pathology and changes in the pathogenesis of cerebral circulation disorders.

Table 4.6.

Reliability of statistical differences in mean values of the coagulogram in patients in primary and control groups with ischemic strokes

Coagulogram indicators	**Main group (n=137),M±m**	**Control group (n=40),M±m**	**Styudent t-criterion (P**
	0,99±0,32	1,14±0,16	0,171
ACHTV/APTV	91,58±2,37	89,3±23,86	0,522
Prothrombin by Quik %	1,20±0,65	1,19±0,47	0,980
MHO	15,16±0,56	14,60±1,58	0,231
Thrombin time, SEC.	95,11±1,90	101,5±0,01	0,001
Antithrombin III, %	4,67±0,17	3,74±0,13	0,0001

Note: M is the middle arithmetic value, m is the standard deviation, n is the number of patients

In addition, patients in the main group with ischemic and hemorrhagic strokes showed a much higher result in fibrinogen levels. Increased Fibrinogen levels not only reflect the activity of the coagulation system, but also serve as a sign of inflammation that will be mentioned in the future. As a result, hypercoagulation syndrome is the most common coagulopathic syndrome in ischemic and hemorrhagic strokes.

Table 4.7
Reliability of statistical differences in mean values of the coagulogram in patients in primary and control groups with hemorrhagic stroke

Coagulogram indicators	Main group (n=29) M±m	Control group (n=20) M±m	Styudent t-criterion (P
	0,89±0,13	0,93±0,18	0,433
ACHTV/APTV	99,19±3,46	89,73±33,20	0,148
Prothrombin by Quik %	1,05±0,09	1,09±0,47	0,784
MnO	13,72±0.54	14,40±3,42	0,321
Thrombin time, SEC.	96,8±18,42	98,52±17,8	0,412
Antithrombin III, %	4,87±1,85	3,47±0,03	0,004

Note: M – middle arithmetic value, m – standard deviation, n– number of patients

In conclusion, it can be concluded that balance dysbalance between coagulation and anticoagulation Blood Systems is more pronounced in patients with recurrent stroke.

Compared to the coagulogram of patients in the main group with ischemic and hemorrhagic stroke, statistically reliable differences in the amount of thrombin time, the amount of prothrombin both indicators showed the activation of the hemostasis system in hemorrhagic stroke.

Table 4.8

Reliability of statistical differences in mean values of the coagulogram in patients in the main group with ischemic and hemorrhagic strokes

Coagulogram indicators	Ischemia stroke (n=108) M±m	Hemorrhagic stroke (n=29) ,M±m	Student t-criterion (P)
ACHTV/APTV	0,99±0,32	0,89±0,13	0,377
Quick-prothrombin %	91,58±2,37	99,19±3,46	0,036
MNO	1,20±0,65	1,05±0,09	0,356

Thrombin, sec.	15,16±0,56	13,72±0.54	0,038
Antithrombin III, %	95,11±1,90	96,8±18,42	0,180
Fibrinogen, g/l	4,67±0,17	4,87±1,85	0,663

Note: M is the middle arithmetic value, m is the standard deviation, n is the amount of patients

The results of the analysis of the hemostasis system in different age groups of patients are presented(table 4.9).

Table 4.9

The main indicators of hemostasis in patients of different ages of the main group with ischemic and hemorrhagic stroke

Indications of hemostasis	Age group							
	18-44 years		45-59 years		60-74 years		75-90 years	
	IS	GS	IS	GS	IS	GS	IS	GS
1	2	3	4	5	6	7	8	9
ACHTV/APTV	0,86 ± 0,11	0,94 ± 0,08	0,96 ± 0,21	0,98 ± 0,08	1,0± 0,12	0,90± 0,14	1,01 ± 0,39	0,88 ± 0,15
Quick-prothromb	96,26±	111,0±	97,27±	118,0±	92,33±	100,31±	89,03±	95,42±

in %	13,83	9,41	15,87	8,41	28,41	7,69	21,11	12,12
MNO	1,05 ± 0,23	0,98 ± 0,15	1,05 ± 0,22	0,99 ± 0,16	1,19 ± 0,70	1,10 ± 0,06	1,31 ± 0,78	1,07 ± 0,05
1	2	3	4	5	6	7	8	9
Thrombin, sec.	15,34 ± 3,87	15,0 ± 1,54	15,24 ± 3,84	15,0 ± 1,54	15,05 ± 1,64	12,83 ± 0,06	15,04 ± 1,36	15,10 ± 0,95
Antithrombin III, %	96,68 ± 10,95	98,10 ± 19,43	96,44 ± 10,81	98,10 ± 19,43	96,33 ± 11,71	105,33 ± 36,68	92,29 ± 7,43	100,40 ± 8,44
Fibrinogen, g/l	4,85 ± 1,66	4,52 ± 1,18	4,65 ± 1,76	4,52 ± 1,18	4,57 ± 1,88	5,42 ± 2,51	4,64 ± 1,57	4,57 ± 1,54

Note: IS-ischemic stroke; GS-hemorrhagic stroke

Table 4.10.

The main indicators of hemostasis in patients of different ages of the control group with ischemic and hemorrhagic stroke

Indications of hemostasis	Age group							
	18-44 years		45-59 years		60-74 years		75-90 years	
	IS	HS	IS	HS	IS	HS	IS	HS
ACHTV/APTV	1,04±0,12	0,92±0,12	1,10±0,11	0,89±0,11	1,14±0,08	0,87±0,10	1,13±0,21	0,85±0,12
Quick-prothrombin %	83,62±31,78	100,50±1,5	86,72±21,78	95,50±1,5	91,24±23,58	92,40±1,5	89,66±22,74	90,30±1,4
MNO	1,20±0,47	1,03±0,25	1,19±0,57	1,13±0,28	1,19±0,58	1,18±0,29	1,21±0,39	1,23±0,40
Thrombin, sec.	15,24±2,84	14,40±2,1	16,24±3,74	14,30±2,0	14,84±1,38	14,50±1,9	14,60±1,34	14±1,8
Antithrombin III, %	95,25±12,8	100,30±14,5	95,0±13,8	100,20±13,5	94,32±15,38	100,10±12,1	94,12±9,44	99,0±10,1
Fibrinogen, g/l	4,08±0,68	4,23±1,34	4,00±0,67	4,00±1,24	3,63±0,66	3,53±1,14	3,77±0,69	3,4±9,6

Note: IS-ischemic stroke; HS-hemorrhagic stroks

Table 4.10 shows that coagulogram rates in older age groups correspond to hypocoagulation compared to younger ones. At the same time, the differences in coagulogram indicators in the main and control group of patients of the remaining 3 age groups are statistically ambiguous. In this case, it is necessary to take into account the fact that elderly patients take drugs that affect various directions of the blood coagulation system, and this affects the results of the study. When comparing the incidence of hemostasis for patients with acute chronic diseases and patients without somatic pathology listed above, the following characteristics were identified. Patients with Type 2 diabetes mellitus, as well as a complex of metabolic disorders that make up the metabolic syndrome, have a much higher prothrombin index rate per quiche (p= 0.043 and 0.037). In addition, antithrombin III has low activity in these two subgroups, but this difference is statistically negligible (p>0.05)(table 4.11).

Table 4.11

The main indications for hemostasis in patients in the main group with side somatic pathology

Indications of hemostasis	CF (n=43)	DT (n=10)	CF+ DT (n=3)	MS (n=5)	CF+ MS (n=7)	(n=52)

ACHTV/AP TV	0,93± 0,14	1,09 ± 0,22	0,83 ± 0,04	0,95 ± 0,15	1,20 ± 0,97	0,94 ± 0,16
Quick-prothrombin %	81,45 ± 21,15	99,2 ± 12,98	97,87 ± 6,53	100,30 ±13,99	97,14 ± 20,43	90,06 ± 13,31
MNO	1,45± 0,97	1,06 ± 0,16	1,01 ± 0,06	0,99 ± 0,06	1,14 ± 0,25	1,03 ± 0,15
Thrombin, sec	14,81 ± 1,16	14,52 ± 1,23	15,11 ± 0,17	14,62 ± 1,34	15,09 ± 1,07	15,75 ± 3,18
Antithrombin III, %	96,6± 12,12	94,30 ± 6,44	99,30 ± 2,45	94,85 ± 5,44	95,0 ± 3,48	98,29 ± 11,29
Fibrinogen, g/l	5,87± 1,73	5,08 ± 1,23	4,55 ± 2,09	5,13 ± 2,42	5,07 ± 1,97	4,54 ± 1,52

Note: CF-compartment fibrillation, DT - diabetes Type 2, MS-metabolic syndrome, without p-pathology.

Very little research has been done to reflect the relationship of tserebrovascular pathology to these processes. This in turn does not lead to an increase in procoagulant activity, the differences being statistically negligible (p<0.05). As for the level of Fibrinogen, it is higher in each of the considered pathologies than in the last control group. Diabetes mellitus, a combination of metabolic syndrome with bladder fibrillation, but a statistically significant difference occurs only in cases of bladder fibrillation (p=0.021).

An important basis for stroke pathogenesis is a cascade of inflammatory reactions. Chronic inflammation, detected in the form of increased levels of C-reactive protein and fibrinogen, serves as one of the risk factors for vascular and brain damage. In this regard, attempts to predict the risk of stroke at the level of inflammatory markers, as well as the introduction of immunomodulatory drugs in the complex treatment of patients, have become increasingly of scientific interest. This study analyzed the levels of C-reactive protein, fibrinogen, as well as the severity of inflammatory changes in the clinical examination of the blood of the main and control groups of patients on the day of admission.

Table 4.12

Average values of inflammatory symptoms in patients with recurrent ischemic and hemorrhagic stroke. (On 1-7 days)

Inflammatory markers	**Main group** (n=108)	Control group (n=29)	Student t-criterion

	M±m	M±m	(P)
Leukocyte, Ch-109	7,91±0,29	6,65±0,32	0,002
Monosite, %	7,33±0,49	5,69±0,28	0,002
Basophilus, %	0,93±0,14	0,45±0,08	0,002
Eosinophilus, %	1,97±1,01	3,37±1,69	0,201
Lymphocyte, %	23,54±10,47	25,57±9,62	0,323
Rod-core neutrophil, %	3,19±2,54	2,55±1,73	0,285
Segment nuclear neutrophil, %	65,92±11,08	61,75±10,07	0,053
S-reactive protein, g / l	10,88±1,51	6,86±1,34	0,025
Fibrinogen, g / l	4,67±0,17	3,74±0,13	0,0001

Note: M is the middle arithmetic value, m is the standard ogish, n is the number of patients

As can be seen from the tables, patients in the main group with recurrent ischemic and hemorrhagic stroke have much higher leukocyte levels. With detailed analysis of granulocytic cells, high levels of monocytes and basophils in the main group are considered. This difference is not described in the available literary sources and probably reflects the characteristics of cellular immunity in chronic inflammation, which is a risk factor for strokes. In addition, reliable levels of C-reactive protein binding have been noted with reversibility of cranial circulation. The increase in C-reactive protein bloodcentration is manifested in 4-6 hours and is accompanied by the destruction of tissues that reach their peak in 24-96 hours.

In the main group, fibrinogen levels are much higher. Fibrinogen not only participates in the coagulation cascade, but also serves as an inflammatory marker along with the C-reactive protein(table 4.13).

Table 4.13

Moderate values of inflammatory symptoms in patients with recurrent ischemic and hemorrhagic stroke. (On 7-12 days)

Inflammatory markers	**Main group** (n=108) M±m	Control group (n=29) M±m	Styudent t-criterion (P)
Leukocyte, Ch109	9,30±1,04	5,93±0,69	0,008
Monosite, %	9,50±0,7	4,50±2,07	0,004
Basophilus, %	0,79±0,42	0,70±0,35	0,892
Eosinophilus, %	1,79±1,05	2,50±0,7	0,449
Lymphocyte, %	23,38±12,99	21,50±9,19	0,847
Rod-core neutrophil, %	4,91±1,16	2,00±0,01	0,014

Segment nuclear neutrophil, %	67,00±10,92	64,50±9,19	0,761
C-reactive protein, g / l	6,88±0,97	4,30±0,0	0,043
Fibrinogen, g / l	4,87±1,85	3,47±0,03	0,004

Note: M is the middle arithmetic value, m is the standard deviation, n is the number of patients

According to the results of the studies, the blood centration of fibrinogen and reactive proteins is high in relation to the large amount of lesion foci, but no direct correlation has been found. In addition, there are attempts to predict the outcome of strokes depending on the level of fibrinogen. Results obtained by comparing inflammatory signs and leukocyte cell levels in patients with primary and relapsed strokes show the specificity of the development of immune reactions that are susceptible to relapsed tserebrovascular damage. These properties require in-depth study through the use of immunoferment analysis techniques, which suggest that there are new risk factors for subsequent strokes. A comparison of C-reactive protein levels has been made in patients of different ages to take into account the age characteristics of inflammatory reactions that occur in response to the formation of acute focal changes in the brain.

In the core group, patients with relapsed ischemic stroke had a tendency to increase C-reactive protein levels with age, but these results are statistically unreliable. There is no such relationship in the control group.

Table 4.14

C-reactive protein levels in patients with ischemic and hemorrhagic stroke of different ages in the main group

Inflammatory markers	Age-based groups							
	18-44years		45-59years		60-74years		75-90years	
	IS	GS	IS	GS	IS	GS	IS	GS
C-reactive protein	9,78 ± 4,04	4,75 ± 2,58	10,58 ± 5,04	5,85 ± 3,58	11,77 ± 5,03	7,79 ± 5,09	12,53 ± 4,98	6,22 ± 4,17

Note: IS-ischemic stroke; GS-hemorrhagic stroke

4.15.Table

C-reactive protein levels in patients with various young ischemic and hemorrhagic strokes in the control group

Inflammatory markers	Age-based groups							
	18-44 years		45-59 years		60-74 years		75-90 years	
	IS	GS	IS	GS	IS	GS	IS	GS

C-reactive protein	3,34± 1,59	2,3± 0,0	5,34± 1,39	4,3± 0,0	7,42 ±1,49	5,3± 0,0	6,88± 0,59	6,3± 0,0

Note: IS-ischemic stroke; GS-hemorrhagic stroke

A link between C-reactive protein levels and pathogenetic subtypes of strokes has been studied among patients in the core group.

Table 4.16

C-reactive protein levels in patients with various pathogenetic stroke subtypes in the main group

Inflammatory markers	Pathogenetic type of ischemic stroke					HS
	CS	AS	L	H	HDS	
C-reactive protein	14,71 ± 4,72	8,09 ± 4,13	7,08 ± 5,85	7,38 ± 3.59	10,1±0,0	6,88 ± 0,97

Note: HS-hemorrhagic stroke, CS – cardioembolic subtype, AS – atherothrombotic subtype, L – lacunar subtype, H - hemorrheological subtype, HDS-hemodynamic subtype

At the same time, the highest level of this inflammatory marker was reported among patients with cardioembolic stroke, and the atherothrombotic pathogenetic subtype differed statistically reliably from this indicator($p=0.009$). The differences between the remaining subtypes are statistically negligible ($p>0.05$). Patients with cardioembolic strokes may have a large ischemic center size and, as a result, the greatest neurological impairment. A comparison was made to test this hypothesis between the neurological deficient severity and C-reactive protein levels under which the NIHSS aid was evaluated.

You may notice a tendency to increase C-reactive protein levels with increased neurological signs. This trend is confirmed statistically: in patients with minimal to moderate variation, the differences between the sign of inflammation are unreliable (p=0.875), but there is a sharp increase in the level of the C-reactive protein thereafter. (p=0.0029). In turn, moderate to severe changes P=0.0007, correlation analyses between C-reactive protein bloodcentration and the number of NIHSS scores compared to patients in critical and critical condition were conducted, and a very strong direct correlation was found (p=0.6; p<0.05). Based on the results obtained, it is possible to draw conclusions about the prognostic role of inflammatory signs in the complex assessment of the condition of patients during the period of acute stroke.

A lipidogram containing total cholesterol, low density lipoproteins, high density lipoproteins, total triglycerides, atherogenicity coefficient was examined in all patients.

Table 4.17

Reliability of statistical differences in average values of lipidogram indicators in patients with ischemic stroke in the main and control groups

Lipidogram indicators	Main group (n=108) M±m	Control group (n=29) M±m	Styudent t-criterion (P)
Total cholesterol, mmol/l	5,54±0,11	5,08±0,23	0,037
Low density lipoproteids, mmol/l	3,53±0,11	2,86±0,21	0,002
High density lipoproteids, mmol/l	1,24±0,35	1,33±0,36	0,182
Common triglycerides, mmol/l	1,61±0,72	1,50±1,10	0,495
Atherogenicity coefficient	3,59±0,14	2,93±0,21	0,006

Note: M is the middle arithmetic value, m is the standard deviation, n is the amount of patients

In the main group of patients, it can be seen that the average value of total cholesterol, low density lipoproteins and atherogenicity ratio is much higher than the control level.

For the main and control group, the comparative severity of patients with non-norm lipidogram indicators was analyzed. In the core group, 39 (32.5%) patients reported high levels of low-density lipoproteid, 68 patients (56.7%) reported hypercholesterolemia, and 60 (50.0%) reported increased atherogenicity. In the control group, cholesterol levels were observed in 12 (35.3%) patients, low density lipoproteid levels in 5 (14.7%) patients, and increased atherogenicity rates in 12 (35.3%) patients, respectively. Thus, the proportion of observations with dyslipidemia in the main group is much higher.

A comparison of changes in lipidogram indicators was made between the main and control groups of patients, depending on the intake of statins. In the main group, 64 (53.3%) patients were on statins, while under control – 21 (61.8%) patients were on statins.

Obviously, the intake of basic and control groupsid statins leads to a statistically significant decrease in total cholesterol and low-density lipoproteins. However, in the main group, unlike control, when using statins, indicators do not reach reference values, in both groups of statins, most patients received. It can be concluded that in the main group it was possible to choose the wrong dose, which is most likely due to the reduced movement of patients with strokes, the ability to control the lipidogram(table 4.18).

Table 4.18

Reliability of statistical differences in average values of lipidogram indicators in patients in the main group who received and did not receive statins

Lipidogram indicators	Those who received Statin (n=54) M±m	Those who did not take Statin (n=44) M±m	Styudent t-criterion (P)
Total cholesterol, mmol/l	5,34±0,13	5,81±0,14	0,031
Low density lipoproteids, mmol/l	3,31±0,09	3,65±0,16	0,044
Atherogenicity coefficient	3,28±0,12	3,89±0,08	0,003

Note: M is the middle arithmetic value, m is the standard deviation, n is the amount of patients

Table 4.19

The main indicators of lipidogram in patients of different ages of the main groups with ischemic and hemorrhagic stroke

LI	Age-based groups

LI	18-44 years		45-59 years		60-74 years		75-90 years	
	IS	HS	IS	HS	IS	HS	IS	HS
TCh	5,52±1,2	5,3±1,23	5,62±1,2	5,32±1,23	5,5±1,01	5,56±1,3	5,63±1,12	5,2±0,86
LDL	3,74±1,01	3,6±1,9	3,54±1,01	3,61±1,9	3,43±1,01	3,62±0,91	3,49±1,15	3,35±0,74
AI	3,74±1,57	3,13±1,32	3,64±1,57	3,23±1,32	3,56±1,31	4,07±1±44	3,29±1,35	3,54±0,71

Note: LI - lipidogram indicators, TCh - total cholesterol, mmol / l, LDL - low density lipoproteins mmol / l, AI-atherogenicity index, IS-ischemic stroke; HS-hemorrhagic stroke

Table 4.20.

The main indicators of lipidogram in patients of different ages of control groups with ischemic and hemorrhagic stroke

LK	Age-based groups							
	18-44 years		45-59 years		60-74 years		75-90 years	
	IS	HS	IS	HS	IS	HS	IS	HS
TC	4,4±0,63	7,15±0,91	5,2±1,48	7,15±1,0	5,2±1,38	7,15±0,91	5,05±1,16	4,7±1,6

H								
LDL	2,18±0,19	4,5±1,65	2,98±1,2	4,8±1,55	2,92±1,1	4,5±1,65	2,93±0,86	2,66±1,7
AI	2,5±1,18	4,39±1,12	2,6±1,1	4,49±1,22	2,7±1,1	4,39±1,12	3,01±0,75	2,88±1,3

Note: LI - lipidogram indicators, TCH - total cholesterol, mmol/l, LDL - low density lipoproteins mmol/l, AI-atherogenicity index, IS-ischemic stroke; HS – hemorrhagic stroke.

No statistically significant differences were found between age groups. Cholesterol levels do not directly depend on age, but increase with the development of a complex of metabolic disorders that are foci on the elderly.

High mean values of lipidogram indicators characterizing the high risk of atherosclerotic vascular changes have been observed in patients with relapsed atherothrombotic ischemic stroke. Reliable differences were found in comparison of total cholesterol ($p=0.003$) and low density lipoproteins ($p=0.015$) levels in atherothrombotic and lacunar stroke. This corresponds, first of all, to the opinions that atherosclerosis is a leading factor in the development of the atherosclerotic subtype in ischemic stroke.

Comparison with lipidogram indicators has been made in patients with and without Type 2 diabetes mellitus in the main group (table 4.21).

Table 4.21

The average value of the main indicators of lipidogram in patients with recurrent ischemic stroke with diabetes mellitus 2 Type

Type 2 diabetes mellitus	TCH P=0,0229 M±m	LDL P=0,0261 M±m	HDL P=0,471 M±m	AC P=0,0013 M±m	AK P=0,043 M±m
Yes (n=82)	5,41±1,07	3,27±1,17	1,2±0,37	1,46±0,51	3,22±1,37
No (n=22)	5,94± 1,1	3,9±1,07	1,21±0,34	1,93±0,98	3.97±1,5

Note: TCH - total cholesterol, mmol / l, LDL-low density lipoproteid, mmol / l, HDL- high density lipoproteid, mmol / l, AC-atherogenicity coeficient, TT - total triglyceride, mmol / l, M-medium arithmetic value, m-standard deviation, n-number of patients

Thus, in the case of diabetes mellitus of the second type in patients is not only an important independent risk factor for blood vessels, but also indirectly affects the occurrence of atherosclerosis. Together, a comparison was made on the spectrum of somatic pathology in groups of patients with primary and recurrent strokes. When hypertension analyzed the characteristics of the disease, it was found that patients with relapsed strokes had a high average blood pressure ($p<0.05$), insufficient dosage of antihypertensive drugs. The role of average blood pressure figures as a risk factor for relapsed stroke has increased with age.

Features of the course of biliary fibrillation were described, the frequency of their occurrence in the main and control group increased in older men. The relative dominance of the taxisistolic form was noted among patients with recurrent stroke, which determines the importance of heart rate control in preventing episodes of cardioembolism. In addition, patients in the main group have a lower need for taking anticoagulants or taking them in low doses. A multi-factor analysis of the causes of relapsed cardioembolic strokes found that the greatest risk was the paroxysmal form of fibrillation.

The incidence of diabetes in the main and control groups increased in women aged 45-56 years. Patients with diabetes mellitus had significantly higher rates of glucose, atherogenicity, and neurological failure severity in relapsed stroke ($p<0.05$).

A comparative analysis of laboratory indicators of patients of the main and control groups was carried out. Comparing signs of inflammation, patients in the main group with recurrent ischemic and hemorrhagic stroke have been found to have leukocyte levels significantly higher than the norm ($p<0.01$). In addition, high levels of C-reactive protein and fibrinogen ($p<0.05$) have been significantly observed with re-disruption of cerebral circulation. These results show the хос nature of the development of immune reactions that are susceptible to relapsed tserebrovascular damage that requires in-depth study. A direct correlation between C-reactive protein levels and neurological deficiency severity levels was found on the NIHSS scale, which made it possible to predict the negative outcome of re-stroke.

The lipidogram evaluation found that the average value of the total cholesterol, low density lipoproteins and atherogenicity coefficient in the main group is much higher than the norm ($p<0.05$). Statistically reliable differences in the evaluation of the hemostasis system have also been obtained: the main group under study recorded high levels of fibrinogen ($p<0.01$) and low levels of antithrombin II ($p<0.01$). Thus, stroke patients have an imbalance between the coagulation and anticoagulant blood systems.

Neurovisual examination methods in stroke patients.

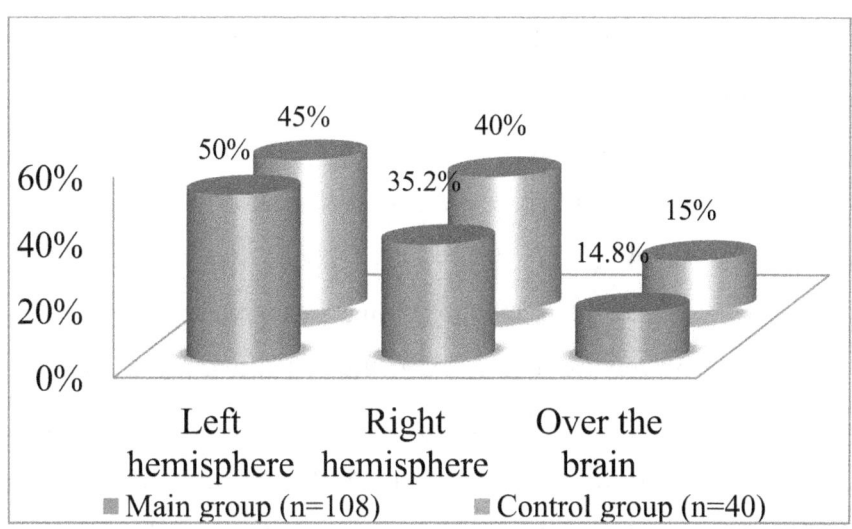

4.1 picture. Localization of the ischemic Center (in%) according to MSKT in stroke patients

As can be seen in Figure 4.1, ischemic strokes in the main group are most often located in the left hemisphere and in the control group-on the right.

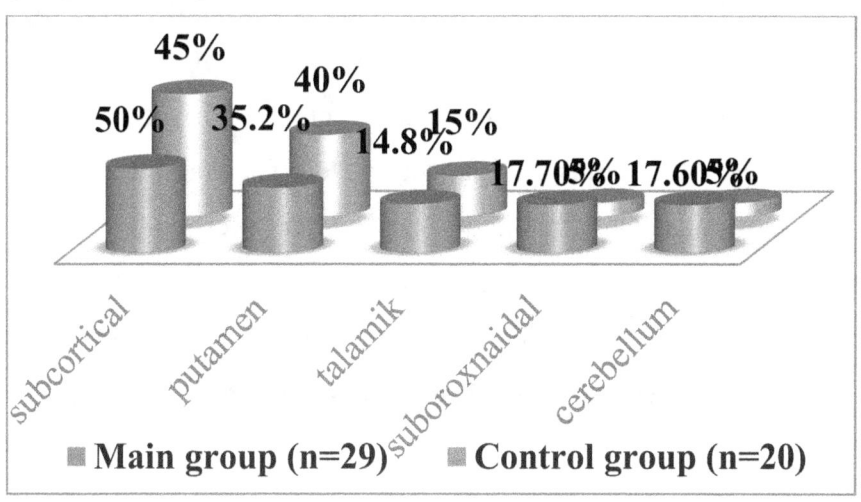

Figure 4.2. Localization of the hemorrhagic Center (in%) according to MRT in stroke patients

In the main group, subcortical bleeding is most common, and in the control group it can be concluded that subcortical, putamen, thalamic bleeding.

Ultrasound diagnosis (duplex angioscaneration with color mapping of the cranial and brachiocephalic arteries, angiospectral Doppler examination) was performed once every 3 days from the day of admission in patients. At the extracranial level, the presence, stability, structure, localization and occlusion levels of atherosclerotic plaques have been assessed in percentage proportions, with the description of pathological residues, ectopic foci. At the intracranial level, the linear rate of blood flow was assessed. In its main group, stenosis is most common – less than 50% in the left internal sleep artery, right and left common sleep artery. In this group, 1 patient was found to have Hemodynamically significant stenosis in the right internal sleep artery, 3 patients – left General sleep artery occlusion, and 4 – right internal sleep artery occlusion.

Table 4.22

Level of stenosis of cerebral arteries according to Duplex and triplex scans of cerebral vessels in the main group (n=120)

Vascular Basin	No stenosis	50% less	50-75%	75-90%	Total occlusion	Total
Left internal sleep artery	75 (62,5%)	32 (26,7%)	10 (8,3%)	0 (0%)	3 (2,5%)	120 (100%)
Right internal sleep artery	85 (70,8%)	22 (18,3%)	8 (6,8%)	1 (0,8%)	4 (3,3%)	120 (100%)
Left common sleep artery	84 (70%)	33 (27,5%)	3 (2,5%)	0 (0%)	0 (0%)	120 (100%)
Right Universal sleep artery	81 (67,5%)	37 (30,8%)	2 (1,7%)	0 (0%)	0 (0%)	120 (100%)
Left external sleeping artery	114 (95%)	4 (3,3%)	2 (1,7%)	0 (0%)	0 (0%)	120 (100%)

Right external sleeping artery	110 (91,5%)	8 (6,8%)	2 (1,7%)	0 (0%)	0 (0%)		120 (100%)
Left vertebral artery	120 (100%)	0 (0%)	0 (0%)	0 (0%)		0 (0%)	120 (100%)
Right vertebral arteriorly	120 (100%)	0 (0%)	0 (0%)	0 (0%)		0 (0%)	120 (100%)
Main artery	120 (100%)	0 (0%)	0 (0%)	0 (0%)		0 (0%)	120 (100%)

When the results were analyzed, it was found that the control group most often had stenosis in the right internal sleep artery, a little less often - stenosis in the right and left common sleep artery. Hemodynamically significant stenosis and occlusions have not been found in the control group.

Table 4.23

According to Duplex and triplex scans of cerebral vessels in the control group, the level of stenosis of the cerebral arteries

Vascular Basin	No stenosis	50% less	50-75 %	75-90 %	Total occlusion	Total
Left internal sleep artery	27 (79,4%)	6 (17,6%)	0 (0%)	0 (0%)	1 (3%)	34 (100%)
Right internal sleep artery	23 (67,6%)	11 (32,4%)	0 (0%)	0 (0%)	0 (0%)	34 (100%)
Left common sleep artery	26 (76,5%)	8 (23,5%)	0 (0%)	0 (0%)	0 (0%)	34 (100%)
Right common sleep artery	26 (76,5%)	8 (23,5%)	0 (0%)	0 (0%)	0 (0%)	34 (100%)
Left external sleeping artery	33 (27%)	1 (3%)	0 (0%)	0 (0%)	0 (0%)	34 (100%)
Right external sleeping artery	33 (27%)	1 (3%)	0 (0%)	0 (0%)	0 (0%)	34 (100%)

Left spinal artery	34 (100%)	0 (0%)	0 (0%)	0 (0%)	0 (0%)	34 (100%)
Right vertebral artery	1 (3%)	0 (0%)	0 (0%)	0 (0%)	0 (0%)	34 (100%)
Main artery	34 (100%)	0 (0%)	0 (0%)	0 (0%)	0 (0%)	34 (100%)

To determine the clinical and pathogenetic properties of relapsed strokes, a comparison of patients of the main and control groups was carried out on a number of parameters. Includes 137 patients with recurrent ischemic (108) and hemorrhagic stroke (29). The ratio of ischemic and hemorrhagic strokes in this group is 4:1. In the control group, 20 patients with ischemic (20) and hemorrhagic stroke were selected. In the control group, the ratio of ischemic and hemorrhagic strokes is equal. At the same time, in old age, patients with a severe recessive neurological deficit are less likely to survive a relapsed stroke. In addition, relapsed strokes for them often lead to death. According to the literature, patients aged 75-90 have a 1.5-fold higher mortality rate with relapsed ischemic stroke. Up to 30% of patients die in the hospital, where about half of patients die in the first 2 days (B.B Fludd, 2008). Statistically significant differences were found when comparing their observations in different age groups with relapsed stroke. There was a neurological impairment between the ages of 74-90 (p<0.01) and less than 45-59 (p<0.05). Thus, the need to use neuroplastic reserves in relapsed strokes affects the viability of the neurological defect formed in patients aged 74-90 years.

4.22 table

Results of α-rhythm indicators in EEG examination of patients

high frequency of α-rhythm	Rehabilitation days	Ipsilateral yamim balloons	Contralateral hemisphere	Norm
F3-F4	5-8 day	6,6±0,8	6,6±3,5	9,5±1,4
	9-12 day	7,3±2,2	8,3±1,1	
	After 12 days	8,9±3,6	9,3±3,2	
C3-C4	5-8 day	4,8±3,3	6,6±4,1	9,5±1,5
	9-12 day	6,9±5,2	8,9±5,9	
	After 12 days	8,7±4,6	9,2±3,3	
T3-T4	5-8 day	4,4±2,4	6,1±3,4	9,8±1,1
	9-12 day	5,6±2,1	8,5±5,1	
	After 12 days	8,2±1,6	9,6±1,6	
O1-O2	5-8 day	6,5±3,2	7,8± 4,3	9,8±1,1
	After 9-12 days	7,7±3,4	8,6±3,4	
	After 12 days	9,5±3,7	9,7±3,1	

Table 4.22 shows that during the most acute period of ischemic stroke, a significant increase in the contralateral hemispheres in the alpha, beta and theta bands was found, a tendency to decrease in the frontal and occipital directions in the Alpha and beta bands, affected hemispheres. all frequency bands were damaged in Alpha and theta rhythms in the temporal pathways and significantly reduced coordination in the contralateral hemispheres. Patients with ischemic stroke have a violation of regional differences: with a sufficiently high connection in the frontal conductors, a high correlation in Alpha rhythm has also been found in the occipital pathways (usually low in the occipital tracts). A general decrease in the contralateral hemisphere and its pathological increase in the low frequency range (Delta and theta) during the acute subsection of ischemic stroke led to disruption of electrical conduction functional connections that provided normal neuropsychic activity of the Cerebral Hemispheres.

In conclusion, the most effective way to prevent embolic complications of arterial fibrillation today is to take anticoagulants. At the same time, only 37.5% of permanent patients and 28.6% of patients with paroxysmal arterial fibrillation took warfarin in the main group. The mean values of MHO were 1.80±1.22, with a target level of 2-3, indicating incorrect selection of the dose of the drug. Multiple analyses have shown that the paroxysmal form of arterial fibrillation has the greatest risk of recurved tserebrovascular pathology in the elderly (p= 0.334). In some cases, the transition of the paroxysmal form to a permanent form can reduce the likelihood of recurrent tserebrovascular pathology, but this decision must be made in conjunction with a cardiologist. 20.8% of patients in the main group and 20.6% of patients in the control group had Type 2 diabetes mellitus in their Anamnesis. Its duration is 20.7±8.1 years in the main group and 18.9±14.3 years in the control group, without statistically significant differences (p>0.05). Diabetes patients with relapsed stroke had significantly higher glucose levels (8.15±2.38 and 5.94±1.29 mmol/l, respectively) (p<0.01) compared to patients without this disease. The difference in atherogenicity coefficient is also recognized as statistically significant (4.07±0.30 and 3.50±0.14, respectively) (p<0.05). The main group of patients with diabetes mellitus have a significantly more pronounced neurological impairment during admission (the NIHSS averages were 12.36 ± 11.58 and 6.13 ± 5.44 points respectively) (p<0.01). Thus, patients with relapsed strokes were combined with diabetes mellitus, deeper metabolic disorders, and severe neurological deficits, consistent with data from other researchers. It should be noted that in 12 patients of the main group, type 2 diabetes mellitus is a component of the metabolic syndrome, combined with dyslipidemia, arterial hypertension and obesity. There were no patients with metabolic syndrome in the control group. It should be noted that in addition to metabolic syndrome, Bulma fibrillation has also been detected in 7 people in the main group. The pathogenetic relationship between olfactory fibrillation and metabolic syndrome has not been sufficiently studied to date, but it is clear that a combination of these pathological conditions significantly increases the risk of circulatory disorders in the brain. This group of patients requires the most careful dispensary monitoring. In addition to differences in pathogenetic scarves and clinical signs, primary and recurrent stroke are characterized by a number of biochemical properties, the knowledge of which allows you to purposefully identify one or another joint in a biochemical cascade, as well as take into account some indicators. Circulatory disorders in the recurrent brain have served as predictors of the disease. Thus, when comparing the parameters of hemostasis in patients in the main and control group, a predisposition to hypercoagulation with a simultaneous decrease in the activity of the anticoagulant system was noted in patients with recurrent stroke. This is evidenced by the low levels of antithrombin III in significant acuity ($95.11 \pm 1.90\%$ in the primary group, $101.5 \pm 0.01\%$ in the control group, respectively) ($p<0.01$), high levels of fibrinogen (4.67 ± 0.17 g). 3.74 ± 0.13 g/l) ($p<0.01$) in the main group and control group, respectively. The data obtained can be used in the development of differential anticoagulant therapy. Modern research defines inflammation as an integral part of the cascade of biochemical reactions corresponding to stroke. The increased activity of inflammatory reactions is characteristic of the elderly and is explained by the fall of the immune system. However, there are no data in the literature on the nature of the IOC to the inflammatory processes themselves of circulatory disorders in the recurrent cranial brain at the age of 45-59 years. A comparison of the symptoms of inflammation in primary and relapsed stroke patients revealed a number of differences. Thus, significantly higher levels of leukocytes have been reported in blood tests of patients in the main group ($6.65 \pm 0.32 \times 109$ versus $7.91 \pm 0.29 \times 109$ in the control group) ($p<0.01$), as well as higher bloodthirsty. C is a reactive protein (10.88 ± 1.51 g/L versus 6.86 ± 1.34 g/l in the control group) ($p<0.05$). These properties indicate the presence of certain properties of the immune state, which are prone to relapsed tserebrovascular pathology. Deep clinical-immuno-biochemical comparisons are required to determine predictions in which cerebrovascular pathologies can recur. In addition, correlation analysis was conducted between C-reactive protein bloodcentration and NIHSS indicator count in the main group of patients, and a very strong direct correlation was found ($p = 0.6$; $p<0.05$). A comparative evaluation of the lipid spectrum in patients in the primary and control group has also found statistically significant differences. Patients with re-stroke have significantly higher total cholesterol levels (5.08±0.23 mmol/l compared to 5.54±0.11 mmol/l in the control group) ($p<0.05$), low density lipoproteins (3.53±0.11 mmol) in the control group respectively 2.86±0.21 versus /l) ($p<0.01$) and atherogenic coefficient (3.59±0.14, respectively in the control group 2.93±0.21) ($p<0.01$). According to our study, dyslipidemia significantly increases the risk of stroke. In the core and control group, patients received statins, but the target lipid profile was not achieved in patients who had suffered a re-stroke. A possible reason is the wrong choice of the dose of the drug, irregular monitoring of blood tests.

CHAPTER V.

Specific characteristics of neurorehabilitation itself in the case after acute circulatory disorders in the recurrent cranial brain.

5.1. Pathogenetic course of relapsed strokes, localization of stroke foci and specific features of neuroreabilitation depending on the structure of neurological deficits

It is advisable to choose neuroreabilitation methods based on the occurrence, pathogenetic type, localization and sex of neurological symptoms. For neuroreabilitation purposes, 137 patients were transferred to the rehabilitation unit. Rehabilitation measures were set individually for each patient. At the same time, an individual was chosen on the floor, taking into account the structure of the neurological deficit, somatic pathology and a number of other factors. The following methods (PSASS, NIHSS, TMT a, TMT V, Bartel scales) were evaluated in order to determine the effectiveness of recovery in patients with re-stroke. As a result, recommendations were developed to manage the rehabilitation process in this category of patients.

The effectiveness of rehabilitation measures in patients with relapses decreased with age, which in turn occurs at the expense of a gradual decrease in tissue potential in neuroglia. Patients with neuroreabilitation had the following age categories: 18-44 years old, 45-59 years old, 60-74 years old, 75-90 years old men had a median age of 72.42 ± 4.6 women with a median age of 73.22 ± 4.32 years. To compare the effectiveness of rehabilitation measures of different ages, the main and control groups were selected.

Table 5.1

Examination scores on the NIHSS scale of patients admitted to the rehabilitation unit

Checked day	Ischemia stroke		Hemorrhagic stroke	
	Primary	Backdated	Primary	Backdated
5-8	12,4±2,2	18,7±1,8	20,2±1,8	22,3±1,7
9-12	10,7±1,8	15,7±2,1	18,3±2,1	20,2±1,9
After 12 days	7,3±1,2	9,3±1,9	10,3±1,1	13,5±1,8

Table 5.2

On the Bartel scale, the average score of patients of different ages is laid in the rehabilitation department and when they come out. Assessment on the Bartel scale

Checked day	Ischemia stroke		Hemorrhagic stroke	
	Primary	Backdated	Primary	Backdated
5-8	22,4±2,2	18,7±1,8	20,2±1,8	12,3±1,7
9-12	38,7±1,8	25,7±2,1	40,3±2,1	28,2±1,9
After 12 days	52,3±1,2	28,3±1,9	60,3±1,1	33,5±1,8

At the same time, many factors that significantly affect the results of neureabilitation measures are associated with the process of age and pathogenetic withdrawal. One of these signs is cognitive, apraxive, sensory impairment. This study analyzes characteristics such as self-control, care, timely execution of exercises said in dynamics, striving to recover, feeling criticism of oneself, depending on the state of attention, speech, perception of patients.

Table 5.3

Average score on the Bartel scale of patients with various cognitive disorders when leaving the reception and Rehabilitation Department

Self-control function	Cognitive distortions on the Bartel scale					
	No cognitive disorders (28-30 points)		Pre-dementia cognitive disorders (24-27 ballov)		Mild degree of dementia (20-23 points)	
	5-8 кун	9-12 кун	5-8 кун	9-12 кун	5-8 кун	9-12 кун
Bartel scale	18,7±1,8	28,3±1,9	14,7±1,7	24,3±1,8	11,7±1,6	25,3±1,7

The average of patients with different cognitive status at the time of leaving the Rehabilitation Unit shows that patients without cognitive disorders and patients with dementia before a re-stroke had approximately the same level of self-care, trying to be good, ability to perform neuroreabilitation exercises. Patients with mild dementia have significantly decreased self-care capacity, and this difference is statistically significant ($p<0.01$). A significantly smaller effect was achieved as a result of rehabilitation measures among patients with mild dementia ($p<0.05$). Thus, cognitive impairment determines the effectiveness of social adaptation and rehabilitation. In addition, this category of patients needs a special approach, mandatory participation of a neuropsychologist in the recovery process. Cognitive rehabilitation strategies have been used when working with patients with impaired cognitive function. The essence of the training in restoring memory, attention and attention was to provide the patient with simple, one-component tasks step by step. Such exercises are designed to activate and restore the individual elements of mental activity necessary for the implementation of more complex forms of purposeful voluntary actions. Patients are involved in training by a neuropsychologist, general practitioner and neurologist, which in turn helps the patient to restore cognitive functions. Performing such exercises will allow the patient to more easily notice and realize all his disorders. As the patient's functionality improves, the gradual complication of tasks and their increase in size, as well as the ability to give the patient positive thoughts and reward and reward even the smallest achievements that he has achieved, remain one of the necessary conditions for training. In the above cases where it is impossible to restore mental function, the patient is taught internal or external strategies to compensate for the functional deficit.

From the manifestation of stroke in terms of early rehabilitation of patients with recurrent stroke, apracto-agnostic and akinetic - rigid syndrome are also noteworthy. Patients who underwent rehabilitation included apracto-agnostic syndrome in 8 cases (13.8%), akinetic-rigid in 4 cases (6.9%). The Rivermed average for patients with apracto-agnostic syndrome was 53.20 ± 7.05, which is statistically much lower than the average for all rehabilitated patients (72.07 ± 19.38) ($p<0.01$). Accordingly, the effects of rehabilitation measures in this group were less pronounced, with a low score of 58.35 ± 6.15, with an average of 81.44 ± 16.05. Dysregulation of Praxis and Gnosis is a factor that causes prognostic discomfort to rehabilitation. Work with patients who have undergone a re-stroke in this category is carried out with the obligatory participation of the doctor. A complex of methods in which Video therapy is used, video discs create clear and unbiased feedback that allows patients to analyze their behavior at any time. Looking at oneself from the outside will allow the patient to better understand its strengths and weaknesses and, when discussing this problem independently, without a doctor, further increase self-confidence. Alternatively, patients with apracto-agnostic syndrome have good results by using videotaped exercises as reflective therapy near the mirror.

In patients with akinetic-rigid syndrome, the average of Rivermid in intake was also much lower statistically, at 56.75 ± 8.43. These disorders increase the manifestation of hemiparesis in patients. In patients, movement skills are restored much more slowly, there is a higher risk of damage during rehabilitation, as well as complications during early recovery (so that complications such as bed sores, hypostatic pneumonia do not arise). In addition, akinetic-rigid syndrome is often accompanied by cognitive impairment and is directly related to blood circulation in the cranial brain. Thus, each of the patients studied had cognitive disorders ranging from mild dementia to 1 dementia. As a result of the rehabilitation measures carried out, a significant positive effect was achieved. This result reduced the burden of patients needing someone's care, allowing them to serve themselves in a home environment. In the process of early rehabilitation treatment of processes such as self-control, self-service of patients with re-stroke do not need the care of someone, special attention was paid to physical therapy sessions with a doctor neuropsychologist, neurologist, wash doctor, the initial skills of proper walking, speaking, correct pronunciation and, among other things, self-service. An important factor determining the development of a blood vessel in the brain of the head is its pathogenetic origin. The comparative effectiveness of rehabilitation measures was analyzed according to the pathogenetic type of stroke. Among patients who underwent rehabilitation treatment, 108 (78.8%) had relapsed ischemic stroke and 29 (21.2%) had relapsed hemorrhagic stroke. 60 patients (55.5%) have cardioembolic subtypes of ischemic stroke, 31(28.7%) are atherothrombotic, 8(7.4%) are lacunar, 2(1.8%) are hemorrhoeological, and 7 (6.6%) reflect the dynamics of neurological status and self - care skills in patients with different pathogenetic subtypes of hemodynamic stroke.

The most obvious neurological defect when admitted to a rehabilitation unit was observed in patients after a cardioembolic stroke. In patients with atherothrombotic stroke, re-strokes were caused against the background of concomitant diseases. The remaining pathogenetic groups are characterized by mild disorders. A much higher effect of rehabilitation in patients with cardioembolic stroke compared to atherothrombotic stroke was found ($p<0.05$). Since there were so many Cardiological nucons, self-care was limited, while the elimination of Cardiological nucons led to a faster recovery of cardioembolic re-strokes. Patients with atherothrombotic stroke recovered more efficiently, due to neuroplasticity, a decrease in the reserve of neurons in the brain tissue, due to the high atherosclerotic process, these patients were confident that the primary damage was small, but these indicators were also low during late rehabilitation. Patients with lacunar stroke initially had minimal changes, and their recovery recovered completely, giving the most results, since the small size of the lesion furnace in this small type of stroke corresponds to the blood count. Patients with hemorrhagic stroke recovered with statistically good efficacy ($p<0.05$). It is possible that the observation early rehabilitation period was not long enough, and these patients remained in need of delayed rehabilitation due to the IOC characteristics of the disease itself.

Table 5.4

Rates of evaluation using the Rivermed scale of patients admitted to the rehabilitation unit for pathogenetic subtypes of ischemic stroke

independent execution of any arbitrary	Ischemia stroke podtypes					HS
	CS	AS	L	H	HDS	

movements						
Rivermead scale	5,1 ± 1,5	6,3 ± 1,7	7,6 ± 2,8	6,1 ± 2,5	5,1 ± 2,5	5,1 ± 1,5

Note: CS - cardioembolic subtype, AS - atherothrombotic subtype, L – lacunar subtype, H - hemorrheological subtype, HDS - hemodynamic subtype, HS - hemorrhagic stroke.

Table 5.5

Average of patients with different pathogenetic types of stroke when leaving the rehabilitation unit using the Rivermid scale

independent execution of any arbitrary movements	Ischemia stroke podtypes					HS
	CS	AS	L	H	HDS	
Rivermead	15,0 ± 1,5	14,3±1,7	15,0± 2,8	14,1± 2,5	13,1 ± 2,5	12,1 ± 1,5

Note: CS - cardioembolic subtype, AS - atherothrombotic subtype, L – lacunar subtype, H - hemorrheological subtype, HDS - hemodynamic subtype, HS - hemorrhagic stroke.

The next important factor affecting the effectiveness of rehabilitation measures is the relative location of primary and recurrent stroke foci. The vascular pool of relapsed ischemic strokes has been identified: in 46 (42.5%) cases, the stroke is in the left midbrain artery Basin, in 37 (34.2%)-in the right midbrain artery Basin, in 25 (23.3%) cases - in the vertebrobazi Basin .

Neurological symptoms coincided with localization of ischemic focus (speech disorders in 18 patients, opposite hemiparesis in 55, 44 vestibuloataxic syndromes, 48 opposite hemigipesthesia, cognitive disorders of varying degrees in 39 patients).

Within the framework of the study, patients were divided into 3 groups:

- in the first group, primary and recurrent ischemic foci are located in the same hemisphere (20 patients on the right, 32 on the left, 14 on the VBB), while the regression of neurological symptoms after the first stroke is completely healed. At the time of admission, the NIHSS score was 3 to 12 (average, 7.1 ± 2.5) points, Bartel 60 to 85 (average, 73.6 ± 7.9) points, Rivermid 61 to 85 (average, 72.1 ± 7.8) points.

- in the second group, primary and recurrent ischemic foci were also located in the same hemisphere (12 patients on the right, 8 on the left), but after the first shock there was a residual neurological defect. At the time of admission, the NIHSS score was 5 to 16 (average, 11.2 ± 3.2) points, Bartel 50 to 80 (average, 63.7 ± 10.9) points, Rivermid 49 to 77 (average, 60.7 ± 10.4) points. This group is associated with the emergence of a new ischemia zone around glial-atrophic changes that are probably already present, in which the neurological defect is more pronounced.

In the third group of patients, primary and recurrent ischemic foci had different localization (in 11 patients, the first stroke developed in the right hemisphere, 7 relapsed in the left hemisphere, 4 returned VBB, 17 localized in the left hemisphere). Of this, 10 were on the right, 7 were on the vbb return), (14 were on the vbb bulgan, of which 7 were on the groove, 7 were on the CHYASH return) followed by a full recovery after the first shot. On admission, the NIHSS score was 2-8 (average 4.5 ± 2.7), Bartel 75-95 (average, 84.3 ± 8.4), Rivermid 67-88 (average 79.8 ± 8.6). In this group, the neurological defect was the smallest. After rehabilitation measures, the best results were achieved in the first group of patients. NIHSS drop scores are 1 - 6 (average 2.3 ± 2.1), Bartel scores 75 – 100 (average, 90.3 ± 9.5), Rivermid scores 75-90 (average, 82.3 ± 6.7).

In this group of patients, it is possible to restore lost functions due to the involvement of the Ipsilateral hemisphere as a result of the activation of undamaged cranial areas and pathways. The anatomical basis for compensation due to the Ipsilateral side is the intersection of the corticospinal tract. In Group 2 of patients, this effect was not so significant. NIHSS scores 2 - 12 (mean, 7.8 ± 3.4) at drop, Bartel scores 55 - 85 (mean, 84 ± 12.1), Rivermid scores 53 - 81 (mean, 67.7 ± 10.8).

Patients of this group have a lower reserve of temporarily disordered neurons that are morphologically conserved but located in the peripocal zone. In the 3rd group of patients, NIHSS's output score was 1-3 (average 1.5 ± 1.1), Bartel scored 80-100 (mean, 89.4 ± 7.7), Rivermid scored 80 - 90 (mean, 86.5 ± 3.2). In this group of patients, a new ischemic focus was formed in the unbroken hemisphere, which allows the reorganization of cortical areas and the more active use of alternative descent pathways in one hemisphere. In contrast, Ipsilateral hemisphere involvement is less important in restoring impaired function in these patients than in previous groups. The effect of Group 3 rehabilitation measures was less than that of Group 1, but given the minimal initial neurological impairment, the functional outcome was much more positive.

5.6 table

Effectiveness of rehabilitation measures

	I-group	II-group	III-group

	During the reception	Rehabilitation then	During the reception	Rehabilitation then	During the reception	Rehabilitation then
NIHSS	7,1 ± 2,5	2,3 ± 2,1	11,2 ± 3,2	7,8 ± 3,4	4,5 ± 2,7	1,5 ± 1,1
Bartel	73,6 ± 7,9	90,3 ± 9,5	63,7 ± 10,9	84 ± 12,1	84,3 ± 8,4	89,4 ± 7,7
Rivermead	72,1 ± 7,8	82,3 ± 6,7	60,7 ± 10,4	86,5 ± 3.2	82,3 ± 6,7	86,5 ± 3.2

Table 5.7

Results of the Schulte scale in strokes

Checked day	Ischemia stroke		Hemorrhagic strok	
	Primary	Backdated	Primary	Backdated
5-8	1,7±0,1	1,8±0,2	1,8±0,2	1,9±0,1
9-12	1,2±0,3	1,3±0,4	1,3±0,2	1,4±0,2
After 12 days	1,1±0,3	1,0±0,5	1,2±0,2	1,3±0,3

The time for Shulte testing is relatively high in primary ischemic stroke at 5-8 days (1.7±0.1 seconds), 9-12 days (1.2±0.3 seconds), 12 days later(1.1±0.3 seconds), 5-8 days in relapsed ischemic stroke (1.8±0.2 seconds), 9-12 days (1.3±0.4 seconds), 12 days later (1.0±0.5 seconds), and 0.01). When patients with hemmoragic stroke are tested for Shulte Sinam, both primary and secondary have poor outcomes (p<0.05), which leads to a rapid response of patients and decreased ability to concentrate as cerebrovascular insufficiency progresses. The" speech fluency " subtest showed lower rates of literal and categorical verbal assosions in patients examined, but performed poorly in secondary strokes compared to Primary Stroke. (p<0.05).

Thus, other authors have also found that a clear difference in neuropsychological indicators indicating the ability to support attention in primary and relapsed strokes, the rate of formation of complications, and the nature of speech development has been identified A.P. According to the theory of Luria (2012), on the basis of such an appearance of cognitive disorders lies neurodynamic dysfunction, that is, a deficiency of functional block I (deep sections of the brain), which constitutes cognitive activity.

Table 5.8

TMT A and V scale results in relapsed stroke

scale	DAY	5-8	9-12	After 12 days

A	Ischemia stroke	88,1±0,1	68,3±0,2	32,4±0,3
	Hemorrhagic strok	89,2±0,2	65,3±0,1	33,5±0,4
B	Ischemia stroke	273,8±0,2	123,5±03	82,3±0,3
	Hemorrhagic strok	279,3±0,1	134,8±0,2	88,5±0,2

In relapsed strokes, the TMT a test shows relapsed ischemic stroke in 5-8 days (88.1±0.1 seconds), 9-12 days (68.3±0.2 seconds), 12 days later(32.4±0.3 seconds), TMT a test in relapsed hemorrhagic stroke in 5-8 days (89.2±0.2 seconds), 9-12 days (65.3±0.1 seconds), 12 days later(in 33.5±0.4 seconds) the results showed that Ham had a negligible result in both strokes. (p) ($p<0.01$).

In a relapsed ischemic stroke in the TMT V test, the TMT V test is performed in 5-8 days (273.8±0.2 seconds), 9-12 days (123.5±0.3 seconds), 12 days later (82.3±0.3 seconds), the TMT V Test in hemorrhagic stroke in 5-8 days (279.3±0.1 seconds), 9-12 days (134.8±0.2 seconds), 12 days later (88.5±0.2 seconds) higher than ischemic stroke ($p<0.01$).

Table 5.9

TMT A and V shkalfsi results at bizamlik stroke

scale	day	5-8	9-12	After 12 days
A	Ischemia stroke	79,3±0,1	62,9±0,2	29,3±0,2
A	Hemorrhagic strok	80,2±0,1	60,2±0,1	28,1±0,1
Б	Ischemia stroke	262,5±0,3	113,8±0,9	78,1±0,3
Б	Hemorrhagic strok	266,1±0,7	125,6±0,4	80,5±0,6

In primary strokes, the TMT a test shows 5-8 days (79.3±0.1 seconds) in primary ischemic stroke, 9-12 days (62.9±0.2 seconds), 12 days later(29.3±0.2 seconds), 5-8 days (80.2±0.1 seconds) in primary hemorrhagic stroke in TMT a test, 9-12 days (60.2±0.1 seconds), 12 days later (28.1±in 0.1 seconds) the results showed that Ham had a negligible result in both strokes. (p) ($p<0.01$).

In a relapsed ischemic stroke in the TMT V test, the TMT V test is performed in 5-8 days (262.5±0.3 seconds), 9-12 days (113.8±0.9 seconds), 12 days later (78.1±0.3 seconds), the TMT V Test in hemorrhagic stroke in 5-8 days (266.1±0.7 seconds),

9-12 days (125.6±0.4 seconds), 12 days later (80.5±0.6 seconds) higher than ischemic stroke ($p<0.01$).

Thus, the effect of rehabilitation of patients after a relapsed ischemic stroke, if the patient has fully recovered after the first stroke, the recovery after primary and relapsed stroke focus in the same hemisphere of the relapsed will also be maximum. Without complete recovery, the neurological defect was most clearly manifested, the effectiveness of rehabilitation measures was 35-45%.

A recurved ischemic stroke in the opposite hemisphere leads to the least pronounced deficit, but a complete recovery cannot be achieved due to a decrease in neuroplasticity potential.

In all 3 groups, the mechanism of readjustment outweighs the real recovery of function and compensation, which should be taken into account when developing a strategy of measures of rehabilitation measures.

Thus, measures aimed at restoring lost function in the first group of patients are effectively used with the help of VR-virtual therapy, including stimulating the connection between the Cerebral Hemispheres.

In the second Group, great attention was paid to measures aimed at replacing the lost function, including teaching the use of auxiliary tools.

Finally, in the third group, work was carried out aimed at restoring the lost function, including, mainly, the effect on the affected limbs.

5.2. Rehabilitation measures in patients with recurrent stroke who have somatic pathology

It is necessary to take into account somatic diseases that accompany the rehabilitation of patients who have suffered from circulatory disorders in the brain. Decompensation of the pathological process in some cases complicates post-stroke rehabilitation. Incorrect levels of physical activity can lead to circulatory disorders in the left ventricle, which in turn can complicate the post-stroke period or even lead to recurrence of tserebrovascular diseases.

At the same time, the ratio of risk and benefit of rehabilitation measures in patients of this category, as well as their optimal size, has not yet been determined.

Patients undergoing rehabilitation treatment also had somatic disorders at the same time. All patients with hypertension, of which 29 (50.0%) had Stage 2 hypertension and 20 (34.5%) had Stage 3 hypertension. Also, all patients suffered from ischemic heart disease, of which 20 people - tension stenocardia of functional Class 1, 8 people - stenocardia of functional Class 2, 15 (25.9%) myocardial infarction. A persistent form of atrophy fibrillation has been reported in 18

(31.0%) patients. 11 patients (19.0%) had a history of Type 2 diabetes. At the same time, at the time of admission, 21 patients had 2 Syues of the functional class, 17 - 1 Syues of the functional class. All patients are prescribed standard drug therapy: antithrombositive, hypertensive drugs, as well as treatment with anticoagulants, beta-blockers, nitrates, antiarrhythmic, sugar micdorin-lowering drugs, according to the instructions.

In the rehabilitation process, blood pressure, ECG, clinical, biochemical blood tests, coagulogram indicators and ultrasound of the lower mucosa were performed. Rehabilitation measures include: significant increase in blood pressure (180/110 mm. sim. ustini); arterial hypotension 90/60 mm.sim.ust post-hypertonic crisis condition; cardiac arrhythmia: paroxysmal form of arterial fibrillation, extrasystole(number of heart contractions 40 to more than 4 extrasystoles); stenocardia in tension 3, 4 functional classes, stenocardia in a calm state, unstable stenocardia; Sue 3, 4 functional classes; deviations of MnO (2-3); thrombosis and thromboembolism; decompensation of diabetes mellitus in patients receiving anticoagulant therapy. On the basis of the Multidisciplinary Medical Association of the Bukhara region, the Department of neurology and rehabilitation, all patients underwent rehabilitation treatment. The rehabilitation period was 20-40 days. Rehabilitation measures were carried out taking into account the structure of the neurological deficit at the time of admission and the nature of the accompanying disease. Patients were given training with electrostimulation, physiotherapy exercises, acupuncture, speech therapy, neuropsychologist. Also, rehabilitation programs include physiotherapeutic treatments, taking into account bloodtractures: photochromotherapy, laser therapy, magnetotherapy, balneotherapy, peloidterapy, lymphocompression manual massage. Patients who had a re-stroke were given general physiotherapeutic treatments (general HydroMassage baths, dry carbon dioxide baths, electrogalvanic baths), and no mechanical exposure to the paretic limbs (lymphocompression, manual massage) treatments were performed to prevent pathological reallocation. Blood flow, the appearance of" robbery syndrome". No electro - treatments were used for patients with Arterial fibrillation.

Pathological conditions that appeared during the course of conducting rehabilitation measures were assessed: vascular injury; hypertensive crisis; increased shortness of breath; increased swelling of the lower mucosa; attacks of stenocardia; episodes of painless myocardial ischemia recorded in the ECG; extrasystole. It should be noted that during the period of complex rehabilitation, serious negative events were not recorded.

The study compared 3 groups of patients with different diseases. The groups did not include 2 patients with a constant form of arterial fibrillation and a combination of stressed stenocardia, 1 patient with a constant form of arterial fibrillation and a combination of Grade 3 hypertension, 7 patients with a combination of stressed stenocardia and Grade 3 hypertension. The distribution was carried out as follows: the first group included patients who suffered a relapsed cardioembolic stroke against the background of a persistent form of arterial fibrillation. Cardioembolic stroke is a clinically severe type with episodes of recurrent ischemia; when taken, the severity of the neurological impairment in this group was maximized. At the time of admission, the NIHSS score was 4 to 15 (average 10.2 ± 3.4), Bartel 45 to 75 (average, 59.2 ± 14.9), Rivermid 45 to 74 (average, 54.3 ± 12.9). Rehabilitation activities in this group were conducted economically. The effect was less than in the control group, nevertheless, by the end of the rehabilitation course, an expansion of each patient's treatment regimen and self-care skills had been achieved. NIHSS scores 3-10 (average, 6.2 ± 2.7) at drop time, Bartel scores 55-85 (average, 76.3 ± 10.5), Rivermid scores 55-80 (average, 67.0 ± 10.4). During rehabilitation, 7 (46.7%) patients reported adverse events: 3

patients had vascular collapse against the background of verticalization, 1 patient had a stenocardial attack, 1 patient had an episode of painless ischemia in the ECG, 2 patients had extrasystole (one of which had an increased case of shortness of breath). In these patients, rehabilitation measures were temporarily stopped, drug therapy was corrected, further tactics of dosing physical activity were discussed with the cardiologist.

In the second group, the neurological defect was the smallest. At the time of admission, the NIHSS score was 3-8 (mean, 4.3 ± 2.5) points, Bartel 75-90 (mean, 83.1 ± 8.0) points, Rivermid 65-87 (mean 78.7 ± 8.7).

As for this group, physical activity is most carefully determined. Nevertheless, positive results were achieved. The NIHSS score is 1-4 (average, 1.8 ± 0.9) at drop time, Bartel scores 85 -100 (average, 89.8 ± 7.4), Rivermid scores 80-89 (average, 86.1 ± 5.2). In addition to the regression of neurological symptoms, the ush in this group recorded an increase in exercise tolerance: Sue was reported in 8 patients (42.1%) when Class 2 was taken, and at the Exit - 5 (26.3%). 12 patients (63.2%) were found to have adverse effects: 7 had vascular collapse (3 of which had episodes of painless ischemia in the ECG), and 5 had a stenocardial attack. The third group consisted of patients with hypertension with high blood pressure in their Anamnesis (12 people). On admission, NIHSS scores range from 4 - 12 (mean,

7.4 ± 3.3) points, Bartel scores from 60 - 80 (mean, 73.0 ± 11.5), Rivermid scores from 59 - 82 (mean, 72.8 ± 6.7). With appropriate antihypertensive therapy, rehabilitation measures were fully implemented, but with lower effectiveness than the control group. Due to premorbid changes in brain tissue, hypertensive encephalopathy phenomena, the potential of neuroplasticity may decrease. NIHSS scores 2 - 9 (Mean, 5.3 ± 1.8) points at drop, Bartel scores 70 - 85 (mean, 75.8 ± 9.3), Rivermid scores 69 - 88 (mean, 82.3 ± 6.7). During rehabilitation, 5 patients (41.7%) experienced adverse effects: 2 patients experienced vascular collapse against the background of verticalization, 2 patients experienced hypertensive crisis, 1 patient had an episode of painless myocardial ischemia in the ECG.

Algorithm of measures for rehabilitation of patients with recurrent stroke

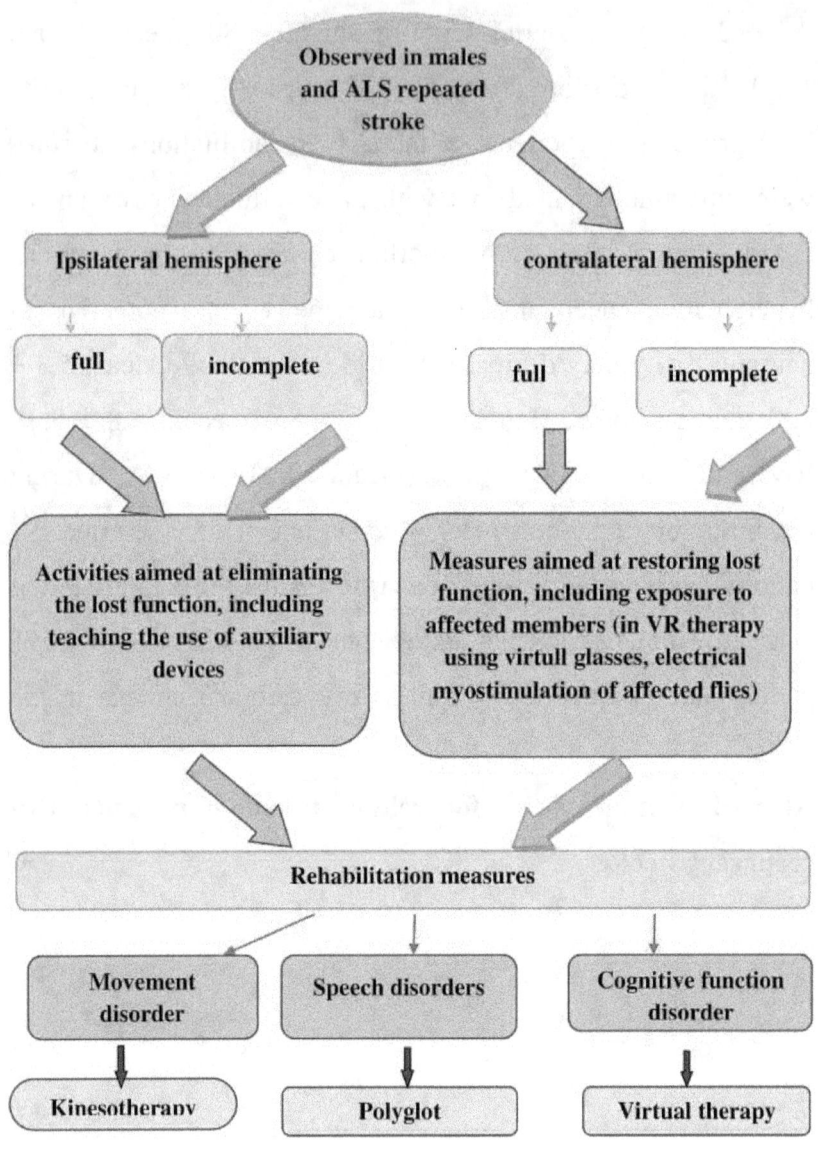

Figure 5.1.Algorithm of measures for rehabilitation of patients with recurrent stroke.

Conclusions

The following conclusions were presented on the basis of research on a monograph on the topic " the effectiveness of early rehabilitation in patients with a re-stroke;

1. In patients with recurrent stroke, clinical and pathogenetic features cardioembolic-50% and atherotrombotic-27% of the high frequency of strokes are detected in 77% of cases, as well as the high level of damage to the left hemisphere of the brain- 45% of patients, the severity of the chronic neurological deficit is more observed in men between the ages of 45-29, primary and re -, but it is characterized by severe clinical course and the predominance of hypertensive bleeding.

2. Relapsed tserebrovascular disorders in male and female patients are associated with hypertension - 80%, cardiac fibrillation - 25%, arrhythmia - 65% after cases and severe course of diabetic angiopathy, which allows them to be classified as etiopathogenetic risk factors for recurrent stroke and is a factor that can be 99% acoc for secondary prevention.

3. Acute circulatory disorders in the recurrent cranial brain occur with more pronounced changes in the hemostasis system (hypercoogulation) and a higher concentration of inflammatory signs ($p<0.05$). On the NIHSS scale, a correlation was established between C-reactive protein concentration and the severity of neurological deficits which was evident at a Mex age of 45-59 years ($p=0.6$; $p<0.05$). These biochemical indicators predicted the outcome of relapsed stroke in 89% of cases.

4. Localization of relapsed stroke foci taking into account the severity of cardiovascular pathalogies and neurological signs, measures for the rehabilitation of male and female patients with relapsed stroke have been developed algorithm that significantly improved the results of treatment in 68-80% of cases.

LIST OF BIBLIOGRAPHY

1. Asrorov A. A., Aminjonová Ch. A. Otsenka sostoyaniya kognitivnix narusheniy u pasientov perenesshix stroke V praktike semeynogo vracha //Central asian journal of medical and natural sciences. – 2021. - c. 397-401.

2. Aleksandrov C.G. Functionalnaya asymmetry I mezhpolusharnie vzaimodeystviya golovnogo mozga: Uchebnoe posobie dlya studentov/ / C. G. Alexandrov; GBOU VPO" IGMU " Minzdrava Rossii, Department normalnoy physiologii.- Irkutsk: IGMU.2014.-C.62.

3. Azin A.L., Yakimova M.E., Kublanov B.C. Ultrazvukovoy analiz I vozmojnost elektroimpulsnoy korreksii izmeneniy v serdechno–sosudistoy sisteme u lis c uskorennim stareniem//Vestnik Uralskoy medisinskoy akademicheskoy nauki. – 2012. – № 3 (40). – C. 48-49.

4. Anaskaya L.H. Osobennosti ishemicheskogo insulta U lyudey pojilogo vozrasta / / medisinskie Novosti. – 2011. – №1. – C. 10-12.

5. Ayrapetov K.B, Aculenoc E.A. , Golovanova E.D frequency vstrechaemosti, stratification riska, techenie I medikamentoznoe lechenie arter alnoy hypertenzii U jentshin v postmenopauzalnom periode// Sciences of Europen № 60.(2020).- C. 9-10.

6. Barantsevich E.P., Conradi A.O., Korostovtseva L.C. Vibor antigipertenzivnogo preparata v osobix gruppax pasientov: Dannie dokazatelnoy mediisini pri soputstvuyutshix zabolevaniyax nervnoy system (chast 5) // arterial. hyperten. – 2015. – № 2. – C. 6-10.
7. Barantsevich E.P., Kovalchuk B.B., Ovchinnikov D.A. Sovremennie vozmojnosti organizasii reabilitasii pasientov posle insulta / / arterial. hyperten. – 2015. – № 2. – C. 96-107.
8. Belova A.H., Prokopenko C.B. Neuroreabilitation . 3–e izd., pererab. I dop. – M., 2011. – C.1288.
9. Belopasova A.B. Organization neuronalnoy rechevoy system u zdorovix lis i ee reorganization u pasientov c postinsultnoy afaziey / A.B. Belopasova [I dr.] / / Annali klinich. I experiment.neurologist. – 2013. - T. 7, № 1. - C. 25-30.
10. Blacklow C.B., Yarchenkova L.L., Kozlova M.B. I dr. Osobennosti vegetativnoy regulyasii U bolnix c razlichnimi formami ishemicheskogo porajeniya mozga // Vulletin of Medical Internet Sonferences. 2014. - T.4,№2. -C. 96.
11. Boytsov C.B., Pakhomova Yu.B., Simonenko B.B. Arterialnaya hypertension V postmenapao'zalnom periode i puti ee terapii / / top med.a – 2009. – № 5. – C.14-17.
12. Burov C.A., Nikitin A.C.Factor riska razvitia zlokachestvennogo techeniya obshirnogo ishemicheskogo stroke / / neurosurgery. – 2012. – № 3. – C. 18-25.

13. Buklina C.B. Narusheniya visshix psychicheskix function pri porajenii glubinnix i stvolovix struct mozga / C.B. Buklina. – M. : Medpress-Inform, 2016. - C. 236-247.

14. Butikov B.H. Kliniko-epidemiologicheskaya characteristic, factor riska I diagnostics, informativnost nekotorix biosimicheskix pokazateley v ostriy period ishemicheskogo stroke: Autoref. dis. ... kand. med. nauk / B.H. Butikov. - Spb., 2011. – C.142.

15. Bikova O.H., Gozeva O.B. Factor riska I preventive ishemicheskogo stroke / / Vestn. Poc. Voen.- med. akad. – 2013. – № 4 (44). – C. 46-48.

16. Ber M., Zikova B.P., Kamchatnova P.P. Neuroprotection: model, mechanism, therapy. Per. C angle. – M.: Binom; lab znani, 2013. – C.429.

17. Varlou Ch.P., Dennis J., Van Geyn J. Stroke. Prakticheskoe rukovodstvo dlya vedeniya bolnix. Per. C angle. - Spb., 2001. – C. 56-64.

18. Verbiskaya C.B. I dr. Postinsultnie cognitivnie narushenia (resolution 5-letnego nablyudenia)//neurology, neuropsychiatry, Psychosomatics. – 2018. - T. 10. – №. 1. – C. 37-42

19. Vachnina H.B., Milovanova O.B. Neurologicheskie rasstroystva U pasientov c arterialnoy hypertensive I IX

correction / / neurology, neuropsychiatry, Psychosomatics. – 2016. – №4. - С.32-37

20. Parfenov B. A., Verbiscaya C. B. Factor riska I prophylactic stroke pri fibrillyasii predserdi/ / neurology, neuropsychiatry, Psychosomatics. – 2014. – №. 3. – С. 55-60.

21. 22. Parfenov B. A., Verbiscaya C. B. Vtorichnaya prophylactic ishemicheskogo stroke I kognitivnix narusheniy / / medisinsky Soviet. – 2016. – №. 11. – С. 18-24.

22. 23. Parfenov B. A., Verbiscaya C. B. Vedenie Bolnogo, perenesshego stroke //neurology, neuropsychiatry, Psychosomatics. – 2013. – №. S2. – С. 23-27.

23. 24. Veretshagin H.B., Djibladze D.H., Gulevskaya T.C. Karotidnaya endarterectomy V prophylactic ishemicheskogo stroke U bolnix C atheroskleroticheskimi stenozami sonnix artery / / jurn. neuropathol. psychiatrist I. im. С.С. Korsakova. – 2017. – № 2. – С. 103-108.

24. 25. Vilensky B.C. Stroke-Spb: Med. Inform. Agentstvo. 2005. – С.287.

25. 26. Voznyuk I.A., Polushin A.Yu., Stepanov E.A.Kolichestvennaya Otsenka ultrazvukovix parametrovmozgovogo krovotoka (znachenie I norma)//regionarnoe krovoobratshenie I microcirculation. – 2013. - Т. 12, № 4 (48). – С. 30-40.

26. 27. Parfenov B. A., Verbiscaya C. B. Postinsultnie kognitivnie narusheniya // medisinsky Soviet. – 2018. – №. 18. – C. 10-15.

27. 28. Voznyuk I.A. Tserebralnaya hemodynamics u lis c nachalnimi proyavleniyami nedostatochnosti krovosnabjeniya mozga: Autoreferat dis. ... kand. med. nauk / I.A. Voznyuk. - Spb., 1994. – C.34.

28. 29. Gafurov B.G., Rachmanova Sh.P. Nekotorie kliniko-pathogeneticheskie characteristic pervogo I povtornogo mozgovikh insultov // mezhdunarodny neurologichesky magazine. – 2011. – №1(39). – C. 59.

29. 30. Gafurov B.G., Roziev Sh.C., Shayzakov A.H.Klinicheskie osobennosti postinsultnix afaziY pri narushenii mozgovogo krovoobratsheniya v dominantnom polusharii u Lis mujskogo I jenskogo Pola//neurology.2012. №3-4.-C.13-15.

30. Gafurov B.G. Izmeneniya EEG pri nekotorixzabolevaniyaxnervnoy system // Klinicheskie lektsii po neurologii. 2016. - C. 107-110.

31. 32. Gafurov B.G., Majidov H.M., Majidova Yo.H. Similar methods of examination in tserebrovascular diseases. Private neurology.2012.-C.28-32.

32. 33. Geraskina L.A. Arterialnaya hypertension I stroke: cardioneurologicheskie aspect vtorichnoy

prophylactic//neurology, neuropsychiatry, Psychosomatics. – 2014. –№ 2. – C. 56-61.

33. 34. Goldobin B.B., Klocheva E.G., Sirotkina O.B. Atherotrombotichesky I lacunarny stroke U pasientov pozhilogo vozrasta: osobennosti klinicheskix proyavleniy I trombositarnogo gemostaza//Uchenie Zapiski Petrozavodskogo gosudarstvennogo universiteta. – 2013. – № 6 (135). – C. 30-35.

34. 35. Goncharova O.A., Parschaladze B.I., Abdullaev P.Ya. Atherosclerosis sonnix artery U bolnix sacarnim diabetom 2 tipa pri normalnoy Masse tela / / Svitmedisinita biologii. – 2014. - T. 10, № 2 (44). – C. 30-32.

35. 36. Gudkova B.B., Usanova E.B., Meshkova K.C. Mozgovoy stroke he bolnix sakharnim diabetom / / effektivnaya pharmacotherapy. – 2014. – № 20. – C. 42-47.

36. 37. Gureeva I.L., Gomzyakowa H.A., Selkin M.D., Isaeva E.P., Golikov K.B. Neuropsychologicheskie izmeneniya u pasientov c ostrim narusheniem mozgovogo krovoobratsheniya/ / Vestnik psychologii-2017-T.10, №4. C.28-36.

37. 38. Didenko L.B. Otdelnie immunologicheskie I bioximicheskie pokazateli u pasientov v rannem vosstanovitelnom periode mozgovix insultov//Ukraïnskiy Journal extremalno ï medisini imeni g.O.Mojaewa. – 2012. - T. 13, № 4. – C. 101-106.

38. 39. Demin D.C., Vasilkiv L.M., Tulupov A.A. Sovremennie vozmojnosti ISPOLZOVANIYA MP-perfuzii pri otsenke tserebralnogo krovotoka//Vestn. Novosibirsk gos. un-ta. Series: biology, Klinicheskaya medisina. – 2015. - T. 13, №4. - C. 47-56.

39. 40. Demografichesky ejegodnik Rossii. 2017: stat.SB. - M. : Rosstat, 2017. – C.263.

40. 41. Dralyuk M.G., Pestryakov Yu.Ya., Dryannix A.A. Rezultati lechenia gemorragicheskogo insulta putamenalnoy lokalizasii po dannim kraevoy klinicheskoy bolnisi g. Krasnoyarska / / Neurosurgery. – 2012. – № 2.– C. 13-16.

41. 42. Dudanov I.P., Pigarevsky P.B., Korzhevsky D.E. Atherosclerosis, sakharny diabetes I autonomnaya innervasia organov serdechno-sosudistoy system//Med. akad.corn. – 2012. - T. 12, № 2. – C. 19-27.

42. 43. Dudanov I.P., Vasilchenko H.O., Laptev K.B. Neurologicheskie iskhodi u pasientov, perenesshix reganstruktivnie operasii na sonnix arteriax, vipolnennix v Ostrom periode ishemicheskogo insulta//Biomedisinsky Journal. – 2011. - T.12, № 7. – C. 873-886.

43. 44. Dudanov I.P., Vasilchenko E.C., Koblov H.O. Hirurgicheskoe lechenie stenozirovannix sonnix artery U pasientov c virajennim neurologicheskim defisitom v Ostrom

periode ishemicheskogo stroke//neurosurgery. – 2013. – № 2. – C. 18-24.

44. 45. Evzelman M.A., Makeeva M.A. Techenie ostrogo ishemicheskogo insulta U bolnix c narusheniem karbabbnogo obmena // jurn. neurol. psychiatrist I. im. C.C. Korsakova. – 2012.– № 2. – C.64-66.

45. 46. Epifanov B.A., Epifanov A.B. Mediko-Sosialnaya reabilitasiya pasientov c razlichnoy pathologiey//BA Epifanov, AB Epifanov-m: Geotar-Media. – 2017. – C. 15-36.

46. 47. Epifanov B.A., Epifanov A.B.Rehabilitation bolnix, perenesshix stroke/ / B.A.Epifanov. - 2-e izd., ISPR. I dop. – M.: Medpress-Inform, 2013. –C. 248.

47. Ekusheva, E.B. K voprosu o mejpolusharnoy asimmetrii v usloviax normi I pathologii / E.B. Ekusheva, I.B. Damolin/ / Corn. neuropath. I psych. – 2014. - T. 114, № 3. - C. 92-97.

48. 49. Ershov B.I., Safronov E. Yu., Chirkov A. H. Oslozhnenny ishemichesky stroke: techenie I prognosis//orenburgsky medisinsky vestnik. – 2016. - T. 4. – №. 1 (13).

49. 50. Ejov B. B. I dr. Sravnitelnaya Effektivnost primeniya dixatelnix trenajerov" Novoe dixanie " dlya medisinskoy rehabilitasii bolnix c tserebralnoy I cardialnoy pathologiey //Vestnik physiotherapii I kurortologii. – 2018. - T. 24. – №. 2. – C. 102-102.//

50. 51. Jivolupov C. A. Sovremenniy klinicheskiy analiz tserebrovaskulyarnix zabolevaniy: uzlovie Voprosi differentialnoy diagnostics I pathogeneticheskogo lechenia / C. A. Zhivolupov, I.H. Samarsev / / Farmateka. – 2012. – №7. – C. 87-94.

51. 52. Jloba A.A., Nikitina B.B. Viyavlenie I lechenie hypergomosisteinemii. Posobie dlya vrachey. - Spb., 2014. – C.40.

52. 53. Zakharov B.B., Vakhnina H.B., Gromova D.O., Tarapovskaya A.A. Diagnostics I lechenie kognitivnix narusheniy posle insulta / / medisinsky Soviet, -2015.- №10.-C. 14-19.

53. 54. Zemlyanov C. A. I dr. Issledovanie structuri motivasii pri povishenii fizicheskoy aktivnosti kak etiopathogeneticheskogo faktora serdechno-sosudistix I komorbidnix zabolevani //Vestnik physiotherapii I kurortologii. – 2018. - T. 24. – №. 1. – C. 111-112.

54. 55. Ibadullaev Z.P., Abdullaeva D.P., Rozimova N.Q., Boltaeva Z.O.Neuropsychological disorders observed in left hemisphere strokes / / neurology. 2011.№4.-C.93-94.

55. 56. Ivanova G.E. Organization rehabilitasionnogo prosessa / / Klin. vestn. Kremlevsk. Med. – 2012. – № 4. – C. 8-10.

56. 57. Ivanova H.E., Kiryanova B.B., Ruslyakova I.A. Rannyaya reabilitasiya bolnix v Ostrom periode povrejdeniya golovnogo i spinnogo mozga // Metodicheskie rekomendasii dlya internov, klinicheskix ordinatorov, vrachey anesteziologov–reanimatologov, neurosurgov, neurologov, vrachey lechebnoy fizkulturi, physiotherapistov. - Spb., 2014. – C. 24.

57. 58. Ivanova H.E., Kiryanova B.B., Mashkovskaya Ya.H. Sovremennie aspect lechenia chronicheskoy ishemii mozga pri ateroskloroticheskom porajenii preserebralnix artery / / jurn. neurol. psychiatrist I. im. C.C. Korsakova. – 2010.– № 10. – C.46-48

58. 59. Isaeva T.B., Lyadov K.B., Shapovalenko T.B. Osobennosti Ranney rehabilitasii pojilix bolnix C cardioembolicheskim insultom / / Vestnik vosstanovitelnoy medisini. – 2011. – № 3. – C. 38-41.

59. 60. Kadikov A.C., Shakhparonova H.B. Prophylactic povtornogo ishemicheskogo stroke/ / Consilium medicum. – 2010, № 3, pril. – C. 30-32.

60. 61. Kadikov A.C., Chernikova L.A., Shakhparonova H.B. Rehabilitation bolnix, perenesshix stroke. Vosstanovlenie motornix, rechevix, cognitivnix functionality. "Trudny pasient 10.11 (2012): 22-27

61. 62. Kazachanskaya E.F. Rannyaya rehabilitation bolnix, perenesshix stroke, V usloviax cardioneurologicheskogo sanatorium: dis. kand. med. nauk. - Samara, 2015. – C.67.

62. 63. Cappepo L. Stroke: program rehabilitasii. – M.: Med. Lit., 2013. – C.160.

63. 64. Kasparov E.B., Gogolashvili H.G., Praxin E.I. Ojirenie, izbitok massi tela I serdechno-sosudistie zabolevaniya (Sovremennie podhodi k preduprejdeniyu urgentnix posledstviy) / /doktor.Ru. – 2012. – № 10

64. (78). – C. 40-42.

65. 65. Kovalchuk V.V. Mediko-Sosialnaya reabilitasiya pasientov posle insulta: Prakticheskoe rukovodstvo. - Spb.; M., 2013. –C. 87.

66. 66. Kotyujinskaya C.G. Pathologicheskie izmeneniya lipid transportnoy system pri saxarnom diabete / / aktualnie problemi transportnoy mediisini. – 2014. - T. 1, № 2. (36). – C. 155-160.

67. Krizhanovsky C.M., Mojarovskaya M.A. Povtorny ishemichesky stroke. Osobennosti taktiki vvedeniya pasientov / / Consilium Medicum. – 2012. - T. 14, № 9. – C. 44-47.

68. 69. Krylov B.B., Lemenev B.L., Murashko A.A. Lechenie pasientov c atheroskleroticheskim porajenie brachiocephalnix artery V sochetanii C intracranialnimi aneurysmami//neurosurgery. – 2013. – № 2. – C. 80-85.

69. 70. Krylov B.B., Dashyan B.G., Lemenev B.L. Hirurgicheskoe lechenie bolnix c dvustoronnimi occlusionno–stenoticheskimi porajeniyami brachiocephalnix arterial//neurosurgery. – 2014. – № 4. – C. 16-25.

70. 71. Krylov B.B. Surgery aneurysm golovnogo mozga, pod Red. B. B. Krylova. – M., 2011. - T. I. –C. 432.

71. 72. Kudukhova E.B. Chronicheskie tserebrovaskulyarnie zabolevaniya na fone metabolicheskogo syndrome: sostoyanie serdechno–sosudistoy system: Autoref. dis. ... kand. med. nauk. – M., 2012. – C.34.

72. 73. Kuznesova C.M., Mankowski H.B., Kuznesova C.M. Vozrastnie izmeneniya neurotransmitternix system mozga kak factor riska tserebrovaskulyarnoy pathologii / / the Journal of Neuroscience. – 2013. - T. 1. – №. 2. – C. 5-13.

73. 74. Kuznesova C.M., Egorova M.C., Skripchenko A.G. Klinicheskie aspect primenenia quercetina u bolnix, perenesshix ishemichesky Stroke / / Journal neurologiï im. BM Mankovskogo. – 2014. – №. 2, № 3. – C. 34-40.

74. 75. Kuznesova C.M. Cardioembolichesky stroke: pathogenesis, clinic, therapy//Zdorove Ukraini. – 2012. - T. 7. – №. 284. – C. 32-34.

75. 76. Kuznesova C.M., Kuznesov B.B. Nasionalno-etnicheskie osobennosti izmeneniy bioelektricheskoy aktivnosti

golovnogo mozga pri starenii//National journal of neurology. – 2013. – №. 3. – C. 115-120.

76. 77. Kuraczyński B.I. Epidemiology sosudistix zabolevaniy golovnogo mozga / / jurn. neurol. psychiatrist I. im. C.C. Korsakova. – 1995. - T. 95, № 2.– C. 4-8.

77. 78. Kuznesova C.M. I dr. Osobennosti tserebralnoy hemodynamiki U bolnix aterotromboticheskim I cardioembolicheskim ishemicheskim insultom v vosstanovitelny period //mejdunarodny neurologicheskiy Journal. – 2011. – №. 2. – C. 18-22.

78. 79. Levin O.C., Bogolepova A.H. Postinsultnie motornie I cognitivnie narusheniya//Journal neurologii I psychiatrii im. C.C. Korsakova 2020, t. 120, No. 11, c. 99-107.

79. 80. Lobzin C.VV., Sokolova M.G., Nalkin C.A. Vliyanie dysfunctsii holinergicheskoy sistemi golovnogo mozgana sostoyanie kognitivnix functionary (obzor literaturi) //Vestnik Severo-Zapadnogo gosudarstvennogo medisinskogo universiteta im. Mechnikova II. – 2017. - T. 9. – №. 4. – C. 53-58. Spb.: Spes. Lit, 2013. –C. 69.

80. 81. Lukyanchikova L.B., Belskaya G.H., Khairutdinova D.F. Multigennayatrombophilia kak factor riska povtornogo stroke / / Neurol. corn. – 2014. - T. 19, № 4. – C. 44-49.

81. 82. Lyang O.B. Prognosticheskoe znachenie febrinogena v Ostrom periode ishemicheskogo insulta: Autoref. dis. ... kand. med. nauk. – M., 2012. – C.26.

82. 83. Madzhidov M.M., Troshin B.D. Do insultnogo tserebrovaskulyarnogo zabolevaniya (diagnostics, lechenie I prophylaxis) – Tashkent, 2015. –C. 320.

83. 84. Medvedev I.H., Kutafina H.B. Aggregasionnaya aktivnost trombositov u zdorovix lis vtorogo zrelogo vozrasta // Fundamentalnie issledovaniya. – 2012. - T. 2, № 8. – C. 362-366.

84. 85. Medvedev I.H., Zavalishina C.Yu., Krasnova E.G. Metodicheskie podhodi k otsenke aggregasii I poverxnostnix svoystv trombositov I erythrositov // Fundamentalnie issledovaniya. – 2014. – № 10. – C. 117-120.

85. 86. Merxols Ya. Rannyaya rehabilitation posle stroke. Per. C angle. pod Red. G.E.Ivanovoy. – M.: Medpress-Inform, 2014. –C. 248.

86. 87. Mongush X.D., Ondar A.B., Chilbakool P.Ch. factor riska I klinicheskie osobennosti povtornix insultov V Respublike Tiva / / Kazansk. med. corn. – 2014. - T. 95, № 2. – C. 199-202.

87. 88. Mumentaler M., Bassetti M., Detweiler K. Differentialny diagnosis V neurologii / / Rukovodstvo po otsenke, classifikasii I differentialnoy diagnostics

neurologicheskix symptomtov. - 4-e izd. – M.: Medpress-Inform, 2014. – C.360.

88. 89. Nadezhdin A.B. Vozrastnie osobennosti narkologicheskix zabolevaniy / / obtshestvennoe psychicheskoe zdorove: nastoyatshee I budutshee. – 2016. – C. 229-230.

89. 90. Neverovsky D.B. Kurenie I ishemichesky stroke / / neurology, neuropsychiatry, Psychosomatics. – 2010. – № 4. – C. 42-47.

90. 91. Nikitin A.C., Burov C.A., Petrikov C.C. Decompressivnaya kraniotomiya U bolnix co zlokachestvennim techeniem massivnogo ishemicheskogo stroke / / neurosurgery. – 2014. – № 3. – C. 23-29.

91. 92. Nikiforov A.C., Gusev E.I. Chastnaya neurology. - 2-e izd., ISPR. I dop. – M.: Geotar-Media, 2013. – C.768.

92. 93. Novikova L.B., Saifullina E.I., Scoromes A.A. Tserebralny stroke: neurovisualization v diagnostics I otsenke effektivnosti razlichnix metodov lechenia. – M.: Geotar-Media, 2012. – C.152.

93. 94. Odinak M.M., Diskin D.E. Klinicheskaya diagnostics V neurologii: Rukovodstvo dlya vrachey. - 2-e izd., ster. - Spb.: Spes.Lit, 2010. – C.528.

94. 95. Parfenov, Vladimir Anatolevich, and Dina Rustemovna Khasanova. "Ishemichesky stroke."(2012): 288-288.

95. 96. Pizova H.B. Nasredstvennie thrombophilii I stroke // corn. neurol. psychiatrist I. im. C.C. Korsakova. – 2013. - №113 (8) – C 76-80.

96. 97. Polushin A.Yu., Odinak M.M., Yanishevsky C.H.Hypergomocysteinemia-predictor tyajesti insulta na fone obshirnosti povrejdeniya mozgovogo vetshestva // Vestn. Poc. Voen.- med. akad. – 2013. – № 4 (44). – C. 89-94.

97. Popova C.A., Bobrova T.A., Shmirev B.I. Porajenie belogo vetshestva golovnogo mozga I pronisaemost hematoentsefalicheskogo barera u mujchin i u jentshin c hypertonicheskoy encephalopatiey // VIII Vserossiysky s'ezd neurologov. - The Wanderer, 2001. – C.32-33.

98. 99. Potapov B.B., Smyalovsky B.E., Smyalovsky D.B. Sostoyanie koronarnogo krovotoka i sokratimosti miokarda u pasientov c narusheniyami mozgovogo krovoobratsheniya na fone multifokalnogo atherosclerosis // jurn. neurol. psychiatrist I. im. C.C. Korsakova. – 2014. - T.114, № 8. – C. 51-52.

99. 100. Putilina M.B., Soldatov M. Tserebralnie stroke V starcheskom vozraste // doctor. – 2006. – № 5. – C. 29-34.

100. 101. Rumyantseva C.A., Stupin B.A., Afanasev B.B. Sovremennie podhodi k korrektsii kognitivnix rasstroystv u bolnix c sosudistoy komorbidnostyu // Rationalnaya pharmacotherapy v cardiologii. 2013. - T. 9, № 2. – C. 123-127.

101. 102. Sagatov D.P., Madzhidova Yo.H. Osobennosti faktorov riska insulta v molodom vozraste // Prakticheskaya neurology I neuroreabilitation. – 2010. – №1. - С. 4-6.

102. 103. Semak A.E., Borisov A.B., Kornatsevich Yu.C. Biochemistry marker belok S100 I SRB v assosiasii C characterom techeniya i ischodom ishemicheskogo insulta//(Literaturny obzor) // Molodoy ucheniy. 2016. № 12 (116). С. 519-522.

103. 104. Semak A.E., Borisov A.B., Lure T.B. Prognozirovanie-put ryosheniya problem mozgovogo stroke // neurology I neurosurgery v Belarus. – 2009. – № 2 (02). – С. 121-133.

104. 105. Skvorsova B.I., Stakhovskaya JI.B., Ayryan H.Yu. Epidemiology insulta v Rossiyskoy Federasii / B.I. Skvorsova, // Consilium medicum. – 2005. - №1, pril. – С. 10-12.

105. 106. Sorokoumov B.A., Savello A.B. Atherosclerosis vnutricherepnix artery: prichini ishemicheskogo stroke, diagnostics I lechenie// neurology, neuropsychiatry, Psychosomatics. – 2014. – № 2. – С. 50-55.

106. 107. Stakhovskoy L.B Klinicheskie rekomendasii po vedeniyu bolnix c ishemicheskim insultom transitornimi ishemicheskimi atakami // Moscow 2015.

107. 108. Stakhovskoy L.B., Kotova C.B. Stroke. Rukovodstvo dlya vrachey-M.: Mia, 2014. – С. 400.

108. 109. Suslina, M.M. Tanashyan. – M.: Med. kniga, 2004. – C. 110.

109. 110. Suslina Z.A., Piradova M.A. Stroke: diagnostics, lechenie, prevention / Pod Red. Z.A. Suslinoy, - M.: Medpress-Inform, 2009. – C.288.

110. 111. Tanashyan M.M. I dr. Myeloproliferativnie zabolevaniya I ishemicheskiy stroke / / Annali klinicheskoy I experimentalnoy neurologii. – 2014. - T. 8. – №. 2. – C. 41-45.

111. 112. Tanashyan M.M., Tshepankevich L.A., Orlov C.B. Hematology I hemostasis u bolnix c ishemicheskim insultom na fone saxarnogo diabeta 2 tipa I metabolicheskogo syndroma // Annali klinicheskoy I experimentalnoy neurologii. – 2014. - T. 8, № 3. – C. 14-20.

112. 113. Tanashyan M.M., Lago O.B., Antonova K.B. Pathology of Tserebrovaskulyarnaya, metabolichesky syndrome I sakharny diabetes: taktika vedeniya pasientov. Uchebno-Metodicheskie rekomendasii. – M.: Media Sphere, 2014. – C. 10-12.

113. 114. Fludd B.B. Prognozirovanie iskhodov ostrix narusheniy mozgovogo krovoobratsheniya u lis pozhilogo I starcheskogo vozrasta: Autoref. dis. ... kand. med. Nauk. - Spb., 2008. – C.156.

114. 115. Fomin I.B., Mareev B.Yu., Ageev F.T. Sakharny diabetes kak etiologicheskaya prichina HCH v evropeyskoy

chasti Rossiyskoy Federasii (issledovanie epoxa – HCH, Hospitalny etap) // Serdechn. nedostat. – 2012. - Т. 13, № 1. – С. 3-8.

115. 116. Fomina-Chetrousova H.A., Bondarenko K.A. Pervichnaya I vtorichnaya prophylactic insultov // medisinsky vestnik Yuga Rossii. – 2012. – № 3. – С. 61-63.

116. 117. Черний В.И., Ельский В.Н., Городник Г.А. Острая церебральная недостаточность. под ред. В.И. Черния. – 4-е изд., испр. и доп. – Донецк: Издатель Заславский А.Ю., 2010. – С.434.

117. 118. Шахпаронова Н.В., Кадыков А.С., Кашина Е.М. Реабилитация больных, перенесших инсульт. Восстановление двигательных, речевых, когнитивных функций // Трудный пациент. – 2012. – Т. 10, № 11. – С. 22–27.

118. 119. Шахпаронова Н.В., Кадыков А.С. Реабилитация постинсультных больных // Медицинский совет. – 2013. – № 4. – С.92–98.

119. 120. Шепанкевич Л.А., Пилипенко П.И., Пикалов И.В. Ишемический инсульт: оценка параметров сосудисто-тромбоцитарного звена гемостаза в остром периоде заболевания// Вестник неврологии, психиатрии и нейрохирургии. – 2011. – № 1. – С 11–13.

120. 121. Широков Е.А. Профилактика инсульта: актуальные проблемы и новые тенденции //РМЖ. – 2013. – Т. 21. – №. 10. – С. 466-469.

121. 122. Щепанкевич Л.А., Вострикова Е.В., Пилипенко П.И. Липидный профиль и методы его коррекции у больных с ишемическим инсультом на фоне сахарного диабета 2 типа // Медицина и образование в Сибири. – 2013. – № 2. – С. 41.

122. 123. Щепанкевич Л.А., Вострикова Е.В., Пилипенко П.И., Ярмощук А.В., Ахундова Л.Э. Характеристика тромбоцитарно–сосудистого гемостаза у больных ишемическим инсультом на фоне сахарного диабета 2 типа // М. – 2012. – № 2. – С. 75.

123. 124. Шпрах В.В., Клочихина О.А., Тушемилов В.В. Эпидемиология и профилактика повторного инсульта в Восточной Сибир //Международный конгресс, посвященный Всемирному Дню инсульта. – 2017. – С. 723-724.

124. 125. Шкловский В.М. и др. Полиморфизм у больных с высоким риском летальности в результате инсульта и тяжелой черепно-мозговой травмы //Молекулярная медицина. – 2013. – №. 2. – С. 46-50.

125. 126. Ючино К., Гротта Д., Острый инсульт. Пер. с англ. под ред. В.И. Сворцовой. – 2–е изд. – М. : ГЭОТАР – Медиа, 2012. – С.256.

126. 127. Ястребцева И.П., Баклушин А.Е., Мишина И.Е. Рекомендации по организации двигательной активности у пациентов с церебральныминсультом на этапе ранней реабилитации. Учебное пособие. под ред. В.В. Линькова. – М.: ИПЦ «Маска, 2014 –С. 116.

127. 128. Яхно Н.Н. и др. Распространенность когнитивных нарушений при неврологических заболеваниях (анализ работы специализированного амбулаторного приема) //Неврология, нейропсихиатрия, психосоматика. – 2012. – №. 2. – С. 30-35.

128. 129. Яхно Н.Н. и др. Лечение недементных когнитивных нарушений у пациентов с артериальной гипертензией и церебральным атеросклерозом (по данным российского мультицентрового исследования «ФУЭТЕ») //Неврологический журнал. – 2012. – Т. 17. – №. 4. – С. 49-55.

129. 130. Rogalski E. et al. Age-related changes in parahippocampal white matter integrity: a diffusion tensor imaging study //Neuropsychologia. – 2012. – Т. 50. – №. 8. – С. 1759-1765.

130. 131. Jauch E.C. et al. Guidelines for the early management of patients with acute ischemic stroke: a guideline for healthcare professionals from the American Heart Association/American Stroke Association //Stroke. – 2013. – T. 44. – №. 3. – C. 870-947.

131. 132. Hart R.G. et al. Rivaroxaban for stroke prevention after embolic stroke of undetermined source //New England Journal of Medicine. – 2018. – T. 378. – №. 23. – C. 2191-2201.

132. 133. Johnston S.C. et al. Ticagrelor and aspirin or aspirin alone in acute ischemic stroke or TIA //New England Journal of Medicine. – 2020. – T. 383. – №. 3. – C. 207-217.

133. Ivan I., Wreksoatmodjo B.R., Darmawan O. hubungan antara riwayat penyakit jantung dengan tangkat keparahan stroke iskemik akut pertama kali //Majalah Kedokteran Neurosains Perhimpunan Dokter Spesialis Saraf Indonesia. – 2019. – T. 37. – №. 1.

134. Firmansyah F., Andayani T.M., Pinzon R.T. Analisis biaya penyakit stroke iskemik //Jurnal Manajemen Dan Pelayanan Farmasi (Journal of Management and Pharmacy Practice). – 2016. – T. 6. – №. 1. – C. 27-34.

135. Bilgili S. ee al. Nitric Oxide and C-Reactive Protein Levels in Ischemic Stroke //Türk Klinik Biyokimya Dergisi. – 2020. – T. 18. – №. 3. – C. 115-120.

136. Priyono A. H., Permana H., Afriani N. Hubungan Kadar Albumin Serum dengan Lama Rawatan Pasien Stroke Iskemik Akut //Jurnal Kesehatan Andalas. – 2018. – T. 6. – №. 3. – C. 552-558.

137. Juraschek S. P. et al. Effects of intensive blood pressure treatment on orthostatic hypotension: a systematic review and individual participant–based meta-analysis //Annals of internal medicine. – 2021. – T. 174. – №. 1. – C. 58-68.

138. Bejot Y. Stroke in the very old: incidence, risk factors, clinical features, outcomes and access to resources–a 22–year population–based study// Cerebrovasc dis. – 2010. –Vol. 29. – P. 111–121.

139. Fonarow G.C. Age–related differences in characteristics, performance measures, treatment trends, and outcomes in patients with ischemic stroke // Circulation. – 2012. – Vol. 121. – P. 879–891.

140. Hein A.M. Neuroinflammation and cognitive dysfunction in chronic disease and agin // J neuroimmune pharmacol. – 2012. – Vol. 7(1). – P 3–6.

141. Jauch E.C., Saver J.L., Adams H.P. Guidelines for the Prevention of Strokein Patients with Stroke and Transient Ischemic Attack. A Guidline for Healthcare Professionals from the American Heart Association //American Stroke Association. Stroke. – 2014. – Vol. 45. – P. 2160–2236.

142. Lee P. Effects of aging on blood brain barrier and matrix metalloproteases following controlled corticвal impact in mice // Exp neurol. – 2012. – Vol. 234 (1). – P 50–61.

143. Pizza V., Agresta A. Neuroinflammation and ageing: Current theories and an overview of the data // Rev recent clin trials. – 2011. – Vol. 6(3). – P 189–203.

144. Seo S.R., Kim S.Y., Lee S.Y. The incidence of stroke by socioeconomic status, age, sex and stroke subtype: a nationwide study in Korea // J prev med public health. – 2014. – Vol. 47 (2). – P 104–112.

145. Starby H. Multiplicity of risk factors in ischemic stroke patients: relations to age, sex and subtype – a study of 2505 patients from the lund stroke register // Neuroepidemiology. – 2014. – Vol. 42 (3). P 161– 188.

146. Van Uden I.W. Diffusion tensor imaging of the hippocampus predicts the risk of dementia the RUN DMC study / I.W. van Uden, A.M. Tuladhar, H.M. van der Holst et.al. // Hum Brain Mapp. – 2016. – Vol.37. – P. 327-337

147. Wang. M. Metabolic, inflammatory, and microvascular determinants of white matter disease and cognitive decline / M. Wang, J. Norman, V. Srinivasan // J. Am J Neurodegener Dis. – 2016. – Vol. 5(5). – P. 171–177.

148. Xufeng Y. Effect of Increasing Diffusion Gradient Direction Number on Diffusion Tensor Imaging Fiber Tracking

in the Human Brain / Y. Xufeng, Y. Tonggang, B. Liang, X. Tian et.al. // Korean J Radiol. – 2015. – Vol.16(2). -P. 410–418.

149. Yang M. Combining diffusion tenor imaging and gray matter volumetry to investigate motor functioning in chronic stroke / M. Yang, Y.R. Yang, H.J. Li et.al. // PLoS One. – 2015, - Vol.12. – P.10-15.60–266.

150. Yang M. Combining diffusion tensor imaging and gray matter volumetry to investigate motor functoning in chronic stroke / M. Yang, Y.R. Yang, H.J. Li et.al. // PLoS One. – 2015, - Vol.12. – P.10-15.

151. Yang S. Voxel-Based Analysis of Fractional Anisotropy in Post-Stroke Apathy / Song-ran Yang, Xin-yuan Shang, Jun Tao, et.al. // PLoS One. – 2015. – Vol.10 (1). – P.116-168.

152. Yilmaz U. Diffusion-weighted imaging in acute stroke / U. Yilmaz // Radiologe.121– 2015. – Vol. 55. – P.771-774.

153. Zhang M. Pontine infarction: diffusion-tensor imaging of motor pathways-a longitudinal study / M. Zhang, Q. Lin, J. Lu et.al. // Radiology. – 2015. – Vol.274(3). – P.841-891.

List of published scientific works

1. Salomova.N.Q., Rakhmatova.C.N. Frequency I Vstrechaemost povtornogo stroke V Uzbekistane // New days in medicine. №3(35)2021.-C.204-207.

2. Salomova N.K., Rachmatova C.N. Porajenie Tsentralnoy I pericheskoy nervnoy system pri novoy coronavirusnoy infektsii // Vestnik Tashkent medisinskoy akademii №2.2021.-C. 39-41.

3. Salomova N.K. Osobennosti techeniya I kliniko-pathogeneticheskaya characteristic pervichnix i povtornix insultov // Central Asian Journal of Medical and Natural Science. 2021.-C. 249-253.

4. Salomova N. Q., Rachmatova C.N. Optimization of early rehabilitation of patients with recurrent ischemic and hemorrhagic stroke // Journal neurologii I neurohirurgicheskix issledovanium. 2021y. Pp. 71-76.

5. Salomova N. Q. Clinical and pathogenetic features of re-strokes// New Day in medicine No. 2(40) 2022 y P.662-665.

7. Salomova N.Q. Rehabilitaion processes in patients with secondary diseases // Mejdunarodnaya nauchno - Prakticheskaya conference "integrasiya v Mir I svyaz nauk" 2021.-C.33-34.

8. Salomova N.Q. // Measures of early rehabilitation of speech disorders in patients with hemorrhagic and ischemic stroke// Europe's Journal of Psychology.2021. Vol. 17(3).-P.185-190.

9. Salomova N.Q., Radjabová G.B. // Diagnostics of night breathing disorders clock and respiratory therapy for copd patients// Europe's Journal of Psychology, 2021 Vol. 17(3).- P-181-184.

10. Salomova N.K. // Effektivnost primenenia psychologicheskix testov dlya diagnostic psychologicheskix rasstroystv u bolnix perenesshix COVID-19.// Central Asian Journal of Medical and Natural Science. 2021.-C. 323-326.

11. Salomova N.Factor K riska tserebrovoskulyarnix zabolevanie I poleznoe svoystvo unabi pri prophylaxis// Oriental renaissance: innovative, educational, natural and social sciences scientific journal february -2022 811-817 PP.

12. Salomova N.Xoc properties of neuroreabilitation itself, depending on the pathogenetic course of K //recurrent strokes, the localization of the stroke furnace and the structure of neurological deficits//

13. Salomova N.K// Features of neurorehabilitation itself depend on the pathogenetic course of repeated strokes, localization of the stroke focus and the structure of neurological deficit / / european jornal of research development and sustainability (ejrds) vol. 3 no. 11, november 2022/8-12

14. Salomova N.K// Risk factors for recurrent stroke / / Polish journal of science N52(2022). 33-35.

15. Salomova N.Q //the practical signaling of speech and thinking in repeated stroke// ScienceAsia 48 (2022): 945-949.

Methodological recommendation:

1. Salomova N.Q., Rachmatova C.N. "Optimization of rehabilitation of patients diagnosed with recurrent ischemic and hemorrhagic stroke". Methodological recommendation. 2021.22 PP.

ABBREVIATIONS

AH-arterial hypertension

AP-arterial pressure

AM.- arteriovenous malpharmasia

ALT-alanintransferase

AT-asparttransferase

VBB-vertebra-basillary basin

ID-internal dormancy

IL-10-interleukin 10

CT-computed tomography

CK-creatinkinase

LDG-lactatdegydrogenase

CLMA-cranial left medial artery

MRI-magnetic resonance imaging

MES-medico-economic standard

AMI - acute myocardial infarction

ACDT-acute circulatory disorders of the brain

CCA-common carotid artery

RMA-right midbrain artery

SB-subaroxnaidal bleeding

MA - midbrain artery

UD-ultrasound diagnosis

ATNF - α-α-tumor necrosis factor

CHF-chronic heart failure

ECG-electrocardiography

EEG-electroencephalography

PSASS-psychic status assessment short scale

NIHSS-National Institutes of Health Stroke Scale

www.ingramcontent.com/pod-product-compliance
Lightning Source LLC
LaVergne TN
LVHW010205070526
838199LV00062B/4501